The **Tax Law** of **Private Foundations**

2020 Cumulative Supplement

Fifth Edition

The **Tax Law** of **Private Foundations**

2020 Cumulative Supplement

Fifth Edition

Bruce R. Hopkins

WILEY

Published by John Wiley & Sons, Inc., Hoboken, New Jersey.
Published simultaneously in Canada.

For general information on our other products and services or for technical support, please contact our Customer Care Department within the United States at (800) 762-2974, outside the United States at (317) 572-3993 or fax (317) 572-4002.

Wiley publishes in a variety of print and electronic formats and by print-on-demand. Some material included with standard print versions of this book may not be included in e-books or in print-on-demand. If this book refers to media such as a CD or DVD that is not included in the version you purchased, you may download this material at http://booksupport.wiley.com. For more information about Wiley products, visit www.wiley.com.

Library of Congress Cataloging-in-Publication Data:
ISBN 978-1-119-51258-5 (main edition)
ISBN 978-1-119-75905-8 (supplement)
ISBN 978-1-119-75903-4 (ePDF)
ISBN 978-1-119-75906-5 (ePub)

Cover design: Wiley
Cover image: © phleum / iStockphoto

Printed in the United States of America

SKY10021552_100220

Contents

Preface

This is the second supplement to accompany *The Tax Law of Private Foundations, Fifth Edition*. The supplement covers events occurring from the middle of 2018 (where the book ended) through the middle of 2020.

Most of the law developments that have occurred during the period reflected in this supplement concern the self-dealing rules, with emphasis on the law concerning indirect self-dealing. The book's treatment of this area of private foundation law has been rewritten and expanded. Particular attention has been accorded the estate administration exception, in part because of two recent significant IRS private letter rulings on the point, plus a ruling on the matter of a foundation's expectancy.

Private foundation law is not frequently the subject of court opinions. One court case emerged during the covered period: the *Dieringer* case. Framed as an estate tax charitable deduction valuation case, the set of facts really is a case study in indirect self-dealing. The case is treated from that perspective in this supplement.

Other interesting private letter rulings during the period include aspects of the mandatory payout rule, the law concerning functionally related businesses and program-related investments, spending for charitable purposes, and the qualified appreciated stock rule.

There was some hope that the proposed Department of the Treasury regulations concerning donor-advised funds would materialize during the period—they are likely to constitute the stuff of a supplement by themselves—but, to date, nothing in that regard has occurred.

A supplement of this nature would not be complete without an update on applicable law generated by the Tax Cuts and Jobs Act. Included in this supplement are summaries of the Treasury Department's and the IRS's proposed regulation on the bucketing and excess compensation tax laws.

Sections have been added summarizing the IRS's rules concerning private foundations' funding of disaster relief programs and the import of the prospective revision of the group exemption rules.

Thanks go to Brian T. Neill, Banurekha Venkatesan, and Elisha Benjamin, at John Wiley & Sons, Inc., for their hard work and invaluable help in connection with preparation of this supplement.

Bruce R. Hopkins

Book Citations

Throughout this book, 14 books by the authors (in some instances, as co-author), all published by John Wiley & Sons, are referenced in this way:

1. Hopkins, *IRS Audits of Tax-Exempt Organizations: Policies, Practices, and Procedures* (2008): *IRS Audits*.

2. Hopkins, *The Law of Fundraising, Fifth Edition* (2013): *Fundraising*.

3. Hopkins, *The Law of Intermediate Sanctions: A Guide for Nonprofits* (2003): *Intermediate Sanctions*.

4. Hopkins, *The Law of Tax-Exempt Organizations, Twelfth Edition* (2019): *Tax-Exempt Organizations*.

5. Hopkins, *Nonprofit Governance: Law, Practices & Trends* (2009): *Nonprofit Governance*.

6. Hopkins, *Nonprofit Law for Colleges and Universities: Essential Questions and Answers for Officers, Directors, and Advisors* (2011): *Colleges and Universities*.

7. Hopkins, *Planning Guide for the Law of Tax-Exempt Organizations: Strategies and Commentaries* (2004): *Planning Guide*.

8. Hopkins, *The Tax Law of Charitable Giving, Fifth Edition* (2014): *Charitable Giving*.

9. Hopkins, *The Tax Law of Unrelated Business for Nonprofit Organizations* (2005): *Unrelated Business*.

10. Hopkins, *The Law of Tax-Exempt Healthcare Organizations, Fourth Edition* (2013): *Healthcare Organizations*.

11. Hopkins, *Tax-Exempt Organizations and Constitutional Law: Nonprofit Law as Shaped by the U.S. Supreme Court* (2012): *Constitutional Law*.

The second, fourth, eighth, and tenth of these books are annually supplemented. Also, updates on all of the foregoing law subjects (plus private foundations law) are available in *Bruce R. Hopkins' Nonprofit Counsel*, a monthly newsletter also published by Wiley.

The **Tax Law** of **Private Foundations**

2020 Cumulative Supplement

Fifth Edition

CHAPTER ONE

Introduction to Private Foundations

§ 1.1   PRIVATE FOUNDATIONS: UNIQUE ORGANIZATIONS

p. 1, first line. *Delete* millions of *and insert:*

over 1.5 million[1]

p. 1. *Delete second paragraph.*

p. 2, note 1. *Change footnote number to* **1.1.**

§ 1.2   DEFINITION OF PRIVATE FOUNDATION

p. 5, note 10. *Insert before period:*

; IRS Revenue Procedure (Rev. Proc.) 2020-5, 2020-1 I.R.B. 241, § 7.03

§ 1.7   OPERATING FOR CHARITABLE PURPOSES

p. 18, carryover paragraph, first line. *Insert footnote following period:*

[88.1]Reg. § 1.501(c)(3)-1(c)(1).

---

[1]The IRS Data Book, 2018 (Pub. 55B) informs that there are, as of the federal government's fiscal year 2018, 1,327,714 recognized charitable and like organizations in the United States, plus 115,778 nonexempt charitable trusts and split-interest trusts and 216 apostolic entities. This number of charitable organizations does not include religious organizations that are not required to seek recognition of tax exemption or entities covered by a group exemption.

p. 18, carryover paragraph, sixth line. *Delete* organizational *and insert* operational.

p. 18, carryover paragraph. *Delete fifth complete sentence, including footnote.*

p. 18, note 89. *Delete text and insert:*

A private foundation has its tax-exempt status revoked for failing to engage in any exempt activities over a long period of time (Community Education Foundation v. Commissioner, 112 T.C.M. 637 (2016), appeal denied because of lack of representation (__ F.3d __ (D.C. Cir. 2018))).

p. 18, note 90. *Delete text and insert:*

In general, Tax-Exempt Organizations § 4.4.

§ 1.9 PRIVATE FOUNDATION SANCTIONS

p. 24. *Change heading to read:*

PRIVATE FOUNDATION LAW SANCTIONS

pp. 24–26. *Delete text following heading on page 24 and through the first complete paragraph on page 26, and insert:*

The federal tax rules pertaining to private foundations[136] are often characterized in summaries as if they are typical laws, in the sense of prescriptions governing human behavior. This is not the case; these rules, comprising portions of the Internal Revenue Code, are tax provisions. Thus, this body of law states that, if a certain course of conduct is engaged in (or, perhaps, not engaged in), imposition of one or more excise taxes will be the (or a) result. For example, there is no rule of federal tax law that states that a private foundation may not engage in an act of self-dealing;[137] rather, the law is that an act of self-dealing will trigger one or more excise taxes and other sanctions.[138]

(a) Sanctions (a Reprise)

Because of the nature of this statutory tax law structure, a person subject to an excise tax does not merely pay it and continue with the transaction and its consequences, as is the case with nearly all federal tax regimes. This structure weaves a series of spiraling taxes from which the private foundation, and/or

---

[136] E.g., § 1.4(a)-(h).

[137] State law, however, may contain such a rule. E.g., Neb. Rev. Stat. § 21-1916.

[138] Even the IRS occasionally gets this wrong. For example, in a private letter ruling, the IRS stated that certain payments by a private foundation to disqualified persons "would be acts of self-dealing that are prohibited by Chapter 42 of the Internal Revenue Code" (Priv. Ltr. Rul. 201703003).

disqualified person(s) with respect to it, can emerge only by paying one or more taxes and correcting (undoing) the transaction involved by paying or distributing assets or having the foundation's income and assets confiscated by the IRS.

The private foundation rules collectively stand as sanctions created by Congress for the purpose of curbing what was perceived as a range of abuses being perpetrated through the use of private foundations by those who control or manipulate them. These provisions comprise Chapter 42 of the Internal Revenue Code. Some of these constraints were placed on supporting organizations and donor-advised funds in 2006.[139]

(b) Self-Dealing Sanctions as Pigouvian Taxes

In the self-dealing context, two excise taxes are imposed on self-dealers—the initial tax[140] and the additional tax.[141] The first tax has a rate of 10 percent; the second a rate of 200 percent. There are also taxes on foundation managers where there is knowing participation in the self-dealing transaction (a scienter requirement).[142] The foundation self-dealing tax subjects the entire amount involved in a self-dealing transaction to tax. Also, the initial self-dealing tax cannot be abated by the IRS.[143] There is the correction feature, by which the self-dealer is required to pay the amount involved to the foundation.[144]

What has come to be known as the *Pigouvian tax* is the brainchild of English economist Arthur Cecil Pigou (1879–1959), a contributor to modern welfare economics. He introduced the concept of *externality* and the belief that externality (social problems) can be corrected by imposition of a tax. A commentator wrote that Pigouvian taxes "aim to regulate behavior by placing a small tax, usually in the form of a uniform excise tax, on the activity to be regulated because of the harm it produces for members of the public."[145]

Does the federal self-dealing tax regime constitute one or more Pigouvian taxes? On the face of it, the answer would seem to be yes.[146] This commentator nicely observed that the self-dealing taxes "have the Pigouvian impulse to protect the public from harm by imposing an excise tax."[147] Despite this impulse, however, three reasons were posited why the self-dealing taxes are

---

[139] See Chapters 15 and 16.

[140] IRC § 4941(a)(1).

[141] IRC § 4941(b)(1).

[142] IRC § 4941(a)(2), (b)(2).

[143] IRC § 4962(b).

[144] IRC § 4941(e)(3).

[145] Aprill, "The Private Foundation Excise Tax on Self-Dealing: Contours, Comparisons, and Character," 17 *Pitt. L. Rev.* 297 (Spring 2020).

[146] This is because of the inherent purpose of these taxes which is to regulate behavior, with the sanctions more in the nature of penalties than taxes (see § 1.9(c)).

[147] Aprill, *supra* note 145, at 329.

not Pigouvian in nature. One, the additional excise tax rate of 200 percent is not "small." Two, the initial tax subjects the entire amount involved in a self-dealing transaction to tax, "even if the transaction benefits the foundation," so that, in those circumstances, the requisite "social costs" are not involved.[148] Third, a Pigouvian tax assumes uniform social costs across all individuals and firms; the commentator mused whether "differences between large and small foundations, between corporate and family foundations, local and national foundations, old and new foundations, etc. should shape the applicable excise tax rules."[149]

Yet, it is understandable why one, perhaps not an economist, would conclude that the self-dealing taxes are Pigouvian in nature, if only because the initial tax cannot be abated and because of the correction requirement. The U.S. Supreme Court stated the general rule about a tax: "Imposition of a tax nonetheless leaves an individual with a lawful choice to do or not do a certain act, so long as he is willing to pay a tax levied on that choice."[150] The self-dealing tax regime does not allow for that type of "lawful choice."

(c) Self-Dealing Sanctions: Taxes or Penalties?

Federal constitutional law differentiates between a tax and a penalty—at least conceptually. This distinction may be drawn in determining whether the exaction passes constitutional muster. A dramatic illustration of this point occurred when a bare majority of the U.S. Supreme Court upheld the constitutionality of the Patient Protection and Affordable Care Act on the basis of Congress's taxing power, construing the health insurance individual mandate (or shared-responsibility payment) as a tax, after the decision was made that the mandate could not be justified as constitutional pursuant to the Commerce Clause.[151] On that occasion, however, the Court observed that "Congress's ability to use its taxing power to influence conduct is not without limits."[152]

In this opinion, the fact that there is a difference between a tax and a penalty was raised, but not resolved. The Court wrote that "there comes a time in the extension of the penalizing features of the so-called tax when it loses

---

[148]*Id.* at ___.

[149]*Id.* at ___.

[150]National Federation of Independent Businesses v. Sebelius, 567 U.S. 519, 574 (2012).

[151]National Federation of Independent Businesses v. Sebelius, 567 U.S. 519 (2012). The Tax Clause is the subject of U.S. Constitution Article I § 8. For a detailed summary of this opinion, see Hopkins, *Tax-Exempt Organizations and Constitutional Law: Nonprofit Law as Shaped by the U.S. Supreme Court* (Hoboken, NJ: John Wiley & Sons, 2012) § 4.8.

[152]National Federation of Independent Businesses v. Sebelius, 567 U.S. 519, 572 (2012).

its character as such and becomes a mere penalty with the characteristics of regulation and punishment."[153] Also, the Court stated that, "[i]n distinguishing penalties from taxes, this Court has explained that 'if the concept of penalty means anything, it means punishment for an unlawful act or omission.'"[154] The Court concluded, having decided that the individual mandate (or shared-responsibility payment) is a tax for constitutional law purposes, wrote that "we need not here decide the precise point at which an exaction becomes so punitive that the taxing power does not authorized it."[155] It should be remembered that, even if an exaction is determined to be a penalty, the constitutionality of the statutory structure may be upheld under the Commerce Clause.[156]

In the opinion, the Court principally relied on two of its precedents in discussing what is and is not a tax. In one of these cases, the Court wrote that a "federal excise tax does not cease to be valid merely because it discourages or deters the activities taxed."[157] It was stated that a tax may have a "regulatory effect" but remains a tax if it "produces revenue."[158] The Court added: "It is axiomatic that the power of Congress to tax is extensive and sometimes falls with crushing effect on businesses deemed unessential or inimical to the public welfare."[159] In the other of these cases, the Court concluded that an ostensible tax was a penalty, because the sanction imposed a heavy burden, included a scienter requirement, and was enforced by a federal agency other than the Department of the Treasury.[160]

The Supreme Court observed, in 1974, that the Court in its "early cases" drew what it saw at the time as distinctions between regulatory and

---

[153] *Id.* at 573.

[154] *Id.* at 567, quoting United States v. Reorganized CF&I Fabricators of Utah, Inc., 518 U.S. 213, 224 (1996).

[155] National Federation of Independent Businesses v. Sebelius, 567 U.S. 519, 573 (2012). Earlier in its opinion, the Court majority held that the payment was not a tax for statutory law purposes.

[156] The shared-responsibility payment was reduced to zero, effective January 1, 2019, by enactment of the Tax Cuts and Jobs Act (Pub. L. No. 115-97, 131 Stat. 2054 (2017). A federal court held that the entirety of the Affordable Care Act, as modified by the TCJA, is unconstitutional because the individual mandate is now unconstitutional because it can no longer be justified as a tax and the mandate is inseverable from the Act's remaining provisions (Texas et al. v. United States, 336 F. Supp. 3d 664 (N.D. Tex. 2018)). An appellate court agreed with the district court as to the present-day unconstitutionality of the individual mandate but remanded the case for a more detailed analysis as to severability (Texas et al. v. United States). The U.S. Supreme Court, on January 21, 2020, declined to expedite its review of this case (U.S. House of Representatives v. Texas, No. 19-841; California et al. v. Texas, No. 19-840). The Fifth Circuit, on January 29, 2020, denied a request for a full-panel hearing of the case (Texas et al. v. United States, No. 19-10011).

[157] United States v. Kahriger, 345 U.S. 22, 28 (1953).

[158] *Id.*

[159] *Id.*

[160] Bailey v. Drexel Furniture, 259 U.S. 20 (1922).

revenue-raising taxes, adding "[b]ut the Court has subsequently abandoned such distinctions."[161] These "early cases" included six court decisions concerning the private foundation law sanctions.

Several court opinions focus on the constitutionality of the federal self-dealing law. In one of these cases, the principal contention was that the provision is an unconstitutional extension of the congressional taxing power.[162] That is, the allegation in that case was that the purpose of the statute is not to raise revenue but to regulate private foundations by imposing penalties on persons who use them for noncharitable, private purposes. The court involved rejected the contention, using five Supreme Court cases as precedent.

The court began its analysis by observing that, in its early decisions analyzing the constitutionality of tax statutes, the Supreme Court "often drew distinctions between regulatory and revenue raising taxes."[163] The court, however, wrote that the Court "has subsequently abandoned such distinctions."[164] The court quoted a 1937 Supreme Court opinion stating that "[i]t is beyond serious question that a tax does not cease to be valid merely because it regulates, discourages, or definitely deters the activity taxed."[165] In that opinion, the Court wrote that this "principle applies even though the revenue obtained is obviously negligible"[166] "or the revenue purpose of tax may be secondary."[167] The Court also stated: "Nor does a tax statute necessarily fall because it touches on activities which Congress may not otherwise regulate."[168] The court concluded that, "[u]nder the present posture of the law, tax statutes are constitutional unless they contain provisions which are extraneous to any tax need."[169]

This court stated that "[i]t is clear that [the self-dealing statute] is constitutional as measured by the standards set forth in [the 1953 case]."[170] It continued: "Congress has seen fit, in enacting the internal revenue laws, to grant tax

---

[161]Bob Jones University v. Simon, 416 U.S. 725, 791, note 12 (1974).

[162]Rockefeller v. United States, 572 F. Supp. 9 (E.D. Ark. 1982), *aff'd per curiam*, 718 F.2d 290 (8th Cir. 1983), *cert. den.*, 460 U.S. 962 (1984).

[163]572 F. Supp. at 13, citing Hill v. Wallace, 259 U.S. 44 (1922); Bailey v. Drexel Furniture Co., 259 U.S. 20 (1922); and Helmig v. United States, 188 U.S. 605 (1903).

[164]Rockefeller v. United States, 572 F. Supp. 9, 13 (E.D. Ark. 1982), quoting United States v. Sanchez, 340 U.S. 42 (1950).

[165]United States v. Sanchez, 340 U.S. 42, 44-45 (1950), citing Sonzinsky v. United States, 300 U.S. 506, 513-514 (1937).

[166]United States v. Sanchez, 340 U.S. 42, 44 (1950), citing Sonzinsky v. United States, 300 U.S. 506, 513-514 (1937).

[167]United States v. Sanchez, 340 U.S. 42, 44 (1950), citing Hampton & Co. v. United States, 276 U.S. 394 (1928).

[168]United States v. Sanchez, 340 U.S. 42, 44 (1950).

[169]Rockefeller v. United States, 572 F. Supp. 9, 13 (E.D. Ark. 1982), citing United States v. Kahriger, 345 U.S. 22, 31 (1953).

[170]Rockefeller v. United States, 572 F. Supp. 9, 13 (E.D. Ark. 1982).

exempt status to certain entities" and "has allowed individuals, corporations, and estates the right to escape taxation of the amounts donated for charitable purposes."[171] "However," the court wrote, "when Congress observed that its legislative grace was being abused, it enacted [the self-dealing statute] to insure that its original intent in granting non-taxable status was complied with."[172] The court concluded that, "[a]lthough [the statute] has a regulatory effect on the activities of charitable organizations and might not raise any revenue, it insures that revenue will be collected under income, estate, and gift tax laws which otherwise might have gone uncollected."[173]

Another court case directly involving a private foundation regulatory provision in relation to the sanction's status as a tax is a challenge to the mandatory payout rule.[174] In that case as well, the argument was that, by enacting the provision, Congress exceeded its power to lay and collect excise taxes. The contention was that the provision does not impose a tax for constitutional law purposes but "imposes a penalty measured by a prescribed rate of return on the value of the foundation's noncharitable property even though the foundation may have no income."[175] The court rejoined that the Supreme Court "has repeatedly rejected this argument," citing the 1928, 1934, and 1937 cases, adding that the "tax in question is a legitimate exercise of the taxing power despite its collateral regulatory purpose and effect."[176]

This court wrote that, "[b]y enacting [the mandatory payout rule] ... Congress decided to subject tax-exempt private foundations to [the rule that the tax must be paid even though the foundation has no income] in order to deal with what it perceived to be an abuse of the foundation's tax-exemption

---

[171] *Id.*

[172] *Id.*

[173] *Id.* The court, in *Rockefeller*, decided that the first-tier self-dealing tax is a penalty for purposes of a rule concerning interest (IRC § 6601(3)). Likewise, Farrell v. United States, 484 F. Supp. 1097 (E.D. Ark. 1980); Deluxe Check Printers, Inc. v. United States, 14 Ct. Cl. 782 (1988), 15 Ct. Cl. 175 (1988), *rev'd on other issue*, 885 F.2d 848 (Fed. Cir. 1989).

Two federal appellate courts rejected the argument that the self-dealing taxes are excise levies and held that these sanctions are penal in nature (Mahon v. United States (In re Unified Control Systems, Inc.), 586 F.2d 1036 (5th Cir. 1978); United States v. Feinblatt (In re Kline), 547 F.2d 823 (4th Cir. 1977)).

Following a brief survey of some of this case law, in a case challenging the constitutionality of the self-dealing excise taxes, the U.S. Tax Court stated simply that it "find[s] no basis for holding any of the provisions of section 4941 unconstitutional (Estate of Reis v. Commissioner, 87 T.C. 1016, 1020 (1986)).

[174] Stanley O. Miller Charitable Fund v. Commissioner, 89 T.C. 1112 (1987). See Chapter 6.

[175] *Id.* at 1119.

[176] *Id.* at 1120. Other tax law arguments rejected in *Miller* are that the mandatory payment tax is a direct tax in violation of Art. 1, sec. 9; and that the tax violates the Sixteenth Amendment. Also rejected was the notion that this form of taxation involves denial of due process in violation of the Fifth Amendment.

privilege," in that "[w]hile donors to the exempt private foundation could receive substantial current tax benefits from their contributions, charity might receive no current benefits because the foundation invested in growth assets that produce no current income but are expected to increase in value."[177] Although the court did not expressly so state, private foundations in this circumstance are required to dip into principal to make the required distribution.[178]

The legislative history of the self-dealing rules is replete with references to the sanctions as penalties. The report of the House Committee on Ways and Means accompanying its version of the 1969 tax legislation states that the "permissible activities of private foundations . . . are substantially tightened to *prevent* self-dealing between the foundations and their substantial contributors."[179] The committee added that it "has determined to generally *prohibit* self-dealing transactions and provide a variety and graduation of sanctions."[180] In this report, there are numerous references to these sanctions as constituting "prohibitions" or arising out of "prohibited" conduct. Identical or similar language appears in the report of the Senate Committee on Finance in connection with its version of the 1969 legislation.[181] This continues to be the view of Congress on this topic, as reflected in a report issued by the Ways and Means Committee in 1996 referring to the private foundation rules as a "penalty regime."[182]

A commentator, following a review of the case law, wrote that the "character" of the self-dealing and similar private foundation provisions "as a tax or a penalty seems uncertain" under the Supreme Court opinion upholding the Affordable Care Act.[183] It is pointed out that the Court's most recent discussion of what constitutes a penalty "turns, at least in part, not on the purpose of or motive for an assessment, but on its level—whether it imposes a heavy burden."[184] Here are the features posed for such a "heavy burden" under the self-dealing sanctions regime: (1) the first-tier taxation of the entire amount of a self-dealing transaction, rather than just the amount by which the foundation is harmed; (2) the second-tier tax rate of 200 percent,

---

[177] Stanley O. Miller Charitable Fund v. Commissioner, 89 T.C. 1112, 1122 (1987).

[178] See § 6.1.

[179] H. Rep. No. 91-413, 91st Cong., 1st Sess. (1969), Part I, at 4 (emphasis added).

[180] *Id.*, Part IV, at 21 (emphasis added).

[181] S. Rep. No. 91-552, 91st Cong., 1st. Sess. (1969).

[182] H. Rep. No. 104-506, 104th Cong., 2nd Sess. 56 (1996). This observation was made in the context of a discussion of the intermediate sanctions rules applicable with respect to public charities, social welfare organizations, and certain nonprofit insurance issuers (IRC § 4958), which in many ways are structured in the same fashion as the private foundation rules. In general, *Intermediate Sanctions*.

[183] Aprill, *supra* note 145, at 322.

[184] *Id.*

which "gives a disqualified person little if any meaningful choice of whether or not to pay the tax"; (3) the implication of the scienter requirement in connection with the excise taxes on foundation managers who knowingly participate in a self-dealing transaction; (4) the court opinions that view the self-dealing sanctions as having the "regulatory purpose [of] rendering self-dealing unlawful"; and (5) the IRS's inability to abate the first-tier excise tax.[185] A sixth indicator of penalty status in this context may be the correction requirement.

This commentator concludes that "private foundation excise taxes do not fit easily into either the category of constitutional taxes or constitutional penalties."[186] As to the self-dealing taxes, the commentator writes that the "status of section 4941 is uncertain under *NFIB*, under the private foundation cases from the 1980s, and the positions of key governmental bodies."[187] Nonetheless, a good case can be made, at least as to the self-dealing tax regime, that the sanctions amount to one or more penalties. The Pigouvian impulse tugs.

(d) Abatement

§ 1.10 STATISTICAL PROFILE

p. 28. *Delete last two paragraphs and insert:*

According to the Foundation Center's data for 2015, the assets of private foundations in the United States totaled $860 billion and qualifying distributions totaled $62.8 billion.

---

[185] *Id.*

[186] *Id.* at 323.

[187] *Id.* at 325.

CHAPTER TWO

Starting, Funding, and Governing a Private Foundation

§ 2.1 CHOICE OF ORGANIZATIONAL FORM

p. 30, note 2. *Delete* IRS Revenue Procedure (Rev. Proc.) *and insert* Rev. Proc.

§ 2.5 ACQUIRING RECOGNITION OF TAX-EXEMPT STATUS

(a) Preparation of Form 1023

p. 41, note 55. *Delete* 2018-5, 2018-1 I.R.B. 235 §§ 4.02 *and insert* 2020-5, 2020-1 I.R.B. 241.

p. 41, second complete paragraph. *Insert as last sentence*:

This application must be submitted to the IRS electronically.[55.1]

(b) Suggestions for Foundation-Sensitive Parts

p. 41, note 55. *Delete Form 1023 Tax Preparation Guide,* Chapter 18;.

p. 47, note 66. *Delete* 2018-5, 2018-1 I.R.B. 235 *and insert* 2020-5, 2020-1 I.R.B. 241.

[55.1]Rev. Proc. 2020-8, 2020-8 I.R.B. 447.

(c) Form 1023-EZ

p. 56, note 92. *Delete* 2018-5, 2018-1 I.R.B. 235 *and insert* 2020-5, 2020-1 I.R.B. 241.

p. 56, first complete paragraph, fifth line. *Delete* 34 *and insert* 25.

p. 56, second complete paragraph, third line. *Insert as third sentence*:

The IRS's procedural rules state that a taxpayer may not rely on, use, or cite as precedent a determination letter issued to another taxpayer.[93.1]

(d) Recognition Application Procedure and Issuance of Determination Letters

p. 56, note 95. *Delete* 2018-5, 2018-1 I.R.B. 235 *and insert* 2020-5, 2020-1 I.R.B. 241.

p. 56, third complete paragraph, fifth line. *Delete* an appeals office *and insert* an office of the Independent Office of Appeals.

p. 57, note 100. *Delete* 2018-5, 2018-1 I.R.B. 235 *and insert* 2020-5, 2020-1 I.R.B. 241.

p. 57, note 101, first line. *Insert id. before existing text.*

p. 58, note 107. *Delete* 2018-5, 2018-1 I.R.B. 235 *and insert* 2020-5, 2020-1 I.R.B. 241.

§ 2.6 SPECIAL REQUIREMENTS FOR CHARITABLE ORGANIZATIONS

p. 61, note 115, last line. *Delete* 2018-5, 2018-1 I.R.B. 235 *and insert* 2020-5, 2020-1 I.R.B. 241.

p. 61, note 116. *Delete* 2018-5, 2018-1 I.R.B. 235 *and insert* 2020-5, 2020-1 I.R.B. 241.

p. 61, note 122. *Delete* 2018-5, 2018-1 I.R.B. 235 *and insert* 2020-5, 2020-1 I.R.B. 241.

§ 2.7 WHEN TO REPORT BACK TO THE IRS

p. 64, carryover paragraph, tenth line. *Insert footnote* 138.1 *following period*:

[138.1]Rev. Proc. 2020-5, 2020-1 I.R.B. 241 §§ 4.02(6), (7).

[93.1]*Id.* § 11.02(1).

(a)   When Should a Ruling Be Requested?

p. 64, fourth complete paragraph, second line. *Delete* $10,000 *and insert* $30,000.

p. 64, note 139. *Delete* 2018-1, 2018-1 I.R.B. 1 *and insert* 2020-1, 2020-1 I.R.B. 1, App. A.

p. 64, note 140. *Delete* 2018-2, 2018-1 I.R.B. 106 *and insert* 2020-2, 2020-1 I.R.B. 106.

(b)   Changes in Tax Methods

p. 65, fifth paragraph, third line. *Delete* $350 *and insert* $6,200.

p. 65, fifth paragraph, third line. *Insert footnote* 142.1 *following comma:*

[142.1]Rev. Proc. 2020-1, 2020-1 I.R.B. 1, App. A.

CHAPTER THREE

Types of Private Foundations

§ 3.1 PRIVATE OPERATING FOUNDATIONS

(c) Individual Grant Programs

p. 93. *Insert following carryover paragraph and before heading:*

A third example of *significant involvement* was provided when the IRS considered a situation involving a private operating foundation with the mission of conducting educational programs assisting underserved and impoverished individuals. The foundation builds the capacity of providers by enhancing their financial sustainability and operational effectiveness. It provides technical assistance to policymakers to support early learning providers, offers technical assistance to enhance use of best practices in childhood development, and conducts research. The foundation proposed to operate a loan program in furtherance of its charitable and educational purposes, including making loans to service providers who cannot qualify for commercial loans; loans may also be made to intermediaries and for-profit entities. Loans to service providers will involve below-market interest rates or be interest-free; loans to for-profit organizations will have below-market rates. The IRS concluded that this foundation will maintain significant involvement in the active programs in support of which the loans will be made. The IRS noted that the foundation employs full-time experts in education and related areas, and funds consultants who specialize in assisting service providers and intermediaries who will receive training, knowledge-sharing, data collection, and educational materials to facilitate capacity-building. The foundation will be involved in the structuring of loans, oversee operations of partners funded with loans, and otherwise plan "substantive elements" with respect to the loan program.[32.1]

(h) Conversion to or from Private Operating Foundation Status

p. 105, first complete paragraph, third line. *Insert footnote* **76.1** *following period:*

> [76.1]Rev. Proc. 2020-5, 2020-1 I.R.B. 241 § 7.04(4).

§ 3.3 CONDUIT FOUNDATIONS

p. 109, carryover paragraph. *Insert footnote* **101.1** *at end of last line:*

> [101.1]The IRS granted an extension of time to a private foundation to make an election under the conduit foundation rules, which is to be timely done by filing an amended annual information return and the requisite statement (Reg. § 301.9100-1), after the firm that prepared the return for the year involved discovered that its calculation of excess distribution carryovers was incorrect (Priv. Ltr. Rul. 201831007).

§ 3.9 FOREIGN PRIVATE FOUNDATIONS

p. 118, note 188. *Insert following existing text:*

A foreign private foundation seeking recognition of exemption as a charitable entity satisfied this 85-percent-support test. This test, however, is not an independent basis for exemption; an organization in this circumstance must, to obtain recognition, meet all the requirements of IRC § 501(c)(3). Thus, this foreign foundation could not be so recognized, in part because it failed the organizational test (see § 1.8) (Priv. Ltr. Rul. 201947020). The organization's defense, which was unavailing, was that the law of the country under which it is organized does not allow alteration of its purposes, so it cannot amend its articles of organization to comply with the test; the foreign rule is based on Stiftung principles, a body of nonprofit law that was largely developed during the Roman Empire and spread throughout Europe.

[32.1]Priv. Ltr. Rul. 201821005.

CHAPTER FOUR

Disqualified Persons

§ 4.1 SUBSTANTIAL CONTRIBUTORS

p. 121, first paragraph, third line. *Delete* appreciate *and insert* appreciation of.

p. 122, first complete paragraph, tenth line. *Delete* provision *and insert* authority.

p. 122, first complete paragraph, eleventh line. *Delete* to calculate *and insert* in calculating.

p. 121, note 2. *Insert as second paragraph:*

The term *disqualified person* is defined somewhat differently in connection with public charities (IRC § 4958(f)). See, e.g., § 4.4, note 60.

p. 123, second complete paragraph, third line. *Delete* or publicly supported.

§ 4.2 FOUNDATION MANAGERS

p. 124, first complete paragraph, first and second lines. *Delete* to mean *and insert* is.

p. 124, second complete paragraph, fifth line. *Delete* precisely.

§ 4.3 CERTAIN 20 PERCENT OWNERS

p. 126, first complete paragraph, first line. *Delete* his or her *and insert* the partner's.

§ 4.4 FAMILY MEMBERS

p. 127, second complete paragraph, fourth line. *Insert* only *following* include.

CHAPTER FIVE

Self-Dealing

§ 5.1 PRIVATE INUREMENT DOCTRINE

p. 138, first complete paragraph, sixth line. *Insert footnote* 12.1 *following period:*

[12.1] An organization was denied recognition of exemption as a charitable entity in part because it issued voting stock providing equity interests to its shareholders, which the IRS found to be a violation of the private inurement doctrine (Priv. Ltr. Rul. 201918020).

p. 140. *Insert as second paragraph:*

The contours of the doctrine of private inurement have been immensely influenced by the intermediate sanctions rules.[23.1] Indeed, in some ways, the intermediate sanctions rules can be viewed as codification of the private inurement doctrine. Disqualified persons are essentially the same as insiders; excessive benefit transactions are much the same as private inurement transactions.[23.2] Developments in the law concerning the intermediate sanctions rules help shape the private inurement doctrine; the reverse is also the case.[23.3]

p. 140, second paragraph. *Delete footnote and insert as last sentences:*

The IRS may, however, resort to application of the private inurement doctrine where there are multiple violations of the self-dealing rules and insignificant grantmaking. For example, the IRS revoked the exempt status of a private foundation on private inurement grounds where it provided a disqualified person with a personal residence, without charge, where the residence was the foundation's only asset and there was little grantmaking.[24] As another illustration, a foundation exemption was revoked where its expenditures were for the personal benefit of its trustees, it did not make any grants, and it did not engage in any other exempt functions.[24.1] Still another illustration was provided in the case of a foundation that engaged in little exempt activity over the audit period.[24.2]

§ 5.2 PRIVATE BENEFIT DOCTRINE

p. 141, carryover paragraph, first complete sentence on page. *Delete and insert:*

Thus, the private benefit doctrine is broader than the private inurement doctrine in the sense that its applicability is not confined to situations involving organizations' insiders but has the potential for applying with respect to any person or person.[30.1]

[23.2]The sanctions, however, are completely different; the intermediate sanctions rules are underlain with excise taxes (as are the self-dealing rules; see §5.15(d)). Also, the intermediate sanctions rules contain exceptions that are not available in the private inurement setting.

[23.3]Developments in both of these areas also help shape self-dealing law; the reverse is also the case.

[24]Tech. Adv. Mem. 9335001.

[24.1]Priv. Ltr. Rul. 201641023.

[24.2]Priv. Ltr. Rul. 201731019.

[30.1]It is an oddity in the law that a doctrine that is based on a few words in a regulation (the private benefit doctrine) can subsume a doctrine that is based on statutory law—indeed, a law that has been in existence for more than 110 years (the private inurement doctrine).

p. 141, carryover paragraph, last sentence. *Delete and insert:*

By contrast, the IRS does not recognize the concept of incidental private inurement.[30.2]

p. 145. *Insert as first complete paragraph:*

Other examples nicely illustrate the extent to which the IRS can apply the private benefit doctrine. A nonprofit corporation, formed to provide training to softball and baseball umpires, and to coordinate and schedule games and tournaments, is also involved in assigning umpires to games and promoting ethical standards among baseball officials; this entity was denied recognition of tax exemption as a charitable or educational organization, in part on the ground that it is serving the private interests of the umpires, who are paid for their services.[52.1] The IRS is ruling that an organization with a small board of trustees or directors is inherently violating the private benefit doctrine, so that a governing board of this nature cannot qualify as an exempt charitable organization.[52.2]

p. 145. *Insert as third complete paragraph:*

As an illustration of incidental private benefit, a tax-exempt charitable organization that allocated Medicaid patients to physicians in private practice was held to provide qualitatively and quantitatively incidental private benefit to the physicians, inasmuch as it was "impossible for this organization to further its exempt purposes without providing some benefit to these physicians."[54.1] Similarly, the IRS ruled that an exempt hospital's investment in a for-profit medical malpractice insurance company, using funds paid by its staff physicians, furthered charitable purposes and was deemed not to extend impermissible private benefit, because the investment was required for the writing of insurance for the physicians, the physicians needed the insurance to practice at the hospital, and the hospital needed the physicians to provide healthcare services to its

---

[30.2] This position, while never particularly credible, is now belied by the fact that the IRS, in the public charity setting, applies the intermediate sanctions rules (see *supra* note 24.1) rather than the private inurement doctrine except in the most egregious circumstances (see *Tax-Exempt Organizations* §§ 20.8, 21.16), thereby causing many acts of private inurement to not result in revocation of tax exemption (and thus be considered forms of incidental self-dealing).

[52.1] Priv. Ltr. Rul. 201617012. This position by the IRS comes close to the proposition that it is a violation of the private benefit doctrine for an organization to use charitable dollars to pay compensation to individuals, either as employees or independent contractors. See, e.g., text accompanied by note 54.1 *infra*.

[52.2] E.g., Priv. Ltr. Rul. 201540019. See *Tax-Exempt Organizations* § 5.7(b). Were this the law (and it is not), there would be few exempt private foundations and perhaps no exempt family foundations.

[54.1] Priv. Ltr. Rul. 9615030.

communities.[54.2] Likewise, the IRS ruled that construction and maintenance of a recreational path on an island was charitable activity, with any resulting private benefit accruing to the residents of the island dismissed as incidental.[54.3] Further, the IRS ruled that a public charity could restore an exempt social club's historic building, where the public would be given substantial access to the facility, with the resulting private benefit to the club and its members regarded as incidental.[54.4]

p. 145, note 52, third line. *Delete text following period.*

p. 145, note 56. *Insert following existing text:*

Unwarranted private benefit was found where a scholarship-granting organization was making grants only to members of one family (and descendants of the founder of the organization); a court condoned revocation of this entity's tax exemption (Educational Assistance Found. for the Descendants of Hungarian Immigrants in the Performing Arts, Inc. v. United States, 111 F. Supp. 3d 34 (D.D.C. 2015) (on appeal)).

p. 150. *Insert following second bullet point and before heading:*

§ 5.3 DEFINITION OF SELF-DEALING

(a) Six Acts

p. 147, note 64, last line. *Insert* federal *following* other.

p. 147, note 64. *Insert as last sentence;*

State law, however, may prohibit self-dealing involving a private foundation.

(b) Statutory Exceptions

p. 148, note 71. *Delete text and insert* See § 5.14(a).

(c) Exceptions Provided in Regulations

p. 149, note 76. *Delete* 5.11 *and insert* 5.12(c).

[54.2]Priv. Ltr. Rul. 200606042.

[54.3]Tech. Adv. Mem. 201151028.

[54.4]Priv. Ltr. Rul. 201442066. On rare occasions, the IRS will find incidental private benefit in circumstances where the benefit may appear, to others, impermissible. For example, the IRS ruled that a public charity may provide its research results to a major for-profit global media corporation for fees, format the information specifically for the company, license rights to derivative works to the company, allow the company to use the charity's information for its internal business purposes, agree to not deliver information to the company's competitors, and agree that the company may have a perpetual license to use the information, with this package of private benefits considered incidental (Priv. Ltr. Rul. 201440023).

p. 150. *Insert following second bullet point:*

- Transactions between private foundations and disqualified persons where the disqualified person status arises only as a result of the transaction.[79.1]

§ 5.3A   EXCESS COMPENSATION TAX

An excise tax of 21 percent is imposed on tax-exempt organizations paying compensation in excess of $1 million, and paying separation amounts, where the employee is one of the five highest-compensated employees.[79.1] The tax base is the *excess* compensation amount.

This tax is imposed on an *applicable tax-exempt organization*,[79.2] which includes conventional tax-exempt organizations.[79.3] Thus, private foundations are applicable tax-exempt organizations. This tax is imposed on *excess* compensation, not necessarily *excessive* compensation, so it is possible that a compensation package can attract both this tax (imposed on the foundation) and a self-dealing tax[79.4] (imposed on the self-dealer).

Compensation of a covered person by a related organization or governmental entity is taken into account for these purposes.[79.5] A person is a *related person* if the person controls or is controlled by the tax-exempt organization,[79.6] is controlled by one or more persons that control the exempt organization, or is a supporting organization[79.7] with respect to the organization.[79.8] The excise tax is prorated among entities paying compensation.[79.9]

Most tax-exempt organizations (and related nonexempt organizations) are unaffected by this law simply because they do not pay any employees remuneration at the level that triggers the tax. That is, there is no excess remuneration[79.10] if an exempt organization (and any related organization) does not

---

[79.1]Reg. § 53.4941(d)-1(a). For example, the bargain sale of property (see *Charitable Giving* § 9.19) to a private foundation is not a direct act of self-dealing if the seller becomes a disqualified person with respect to the foundation only by reason of being a substantial contributor (see § 4.1) as a result of the bargain element of the sale (Reg. § 53.4941(d)-1(a)).

[79.1]IRC § 4960, added by the Tax Cuts and Jobs Act, Pub. L. No. 115-97, 115th Cong., 1st Sess. (2017), § 13602(a).

[79.2]IRC § 4960(c)(1).

[79.3]That is, organizations that are tax-exempt by reason of IRC § 501(a).

[79.4]See § 5.15(d).

[79.5]IRC § 4960(c)(4)(A).

[79.6]The concept of *control* is based on the definition of that term as used in the controlled subsidiary context (IRC § 512(b)(13)(D)) (see *Tax-Exempt Organizations* §§ 29.6, 30.7(d)).

[79.7]See § 15.7.

[79.8]IRC § 4960(c)(4)(B).

[79.9]IRC § 4960(c)(4)(C).

[79.10]IRC § 4960(a)(1).

pay more than $1 million of remuneration to any employee for a tax year and there cannot be an excess parachute payment[79.11] if the employer does not have any highly compensated employees (for 2020, individuals earning more than $130,000[79.12]) for the year.

The government estimates that these proposed regulations will affect about 261,000 exempt organizations and 77,000 nonexempt related organizations. As to these exempt entities, 239,000 are conventional exempt organizations (including 23,000 private foundations),[79.13] 19,000 are state and local governmental entities that have income excluded from taxation,[79.14] 2,000 are political organizations,[79.15] 600 are farmers' cooperatives,[79.16] and the federal instrumentalities involved[79.17] number 200.[79.18]

The Treasury Department and the IRS, in mid-2020, issued proposed regulations concerning the excise tax on excess compensation paid by applicable tax-exempt organizations.[79.19]

A *covered employee* is an individual who is one of the five highest-compensated employees of an applicable tax-exempt organization for a tax year or was a covered employee for a preceding year (beginning in 2017).[79.20] The proposed regulations contain rules for identifying these five highest-paid individuals.[79.21]

Whether an employee is a covered employee is determined separately for each tax-exempt organization. An employee may be a covered employee of more than one exempt organization in a related group of organizations for a year. Once an employee is a covered employee of an exempt organization, the employee continues to be a covered employee of the entity.

Remuneration, for these purposes, does not include the portion of any remuneration paid to a licensed medical professional for medical or veterinary services.[79.22] A substantially similar exception applies in connection with the definition of parachute payment.[79.23]

[79.11] IRC § 4960(a)(2).

[79.12] These individuals are classified as *highly compensated employees* (IRC § 414(q)(1)(B)). The referenced dollar limitation is for 2020 (Notice 2019-59, 2019-47 I.R.B. 1091).

[79.13] That is, organizations that are tax-exempt by reason of IRC § 501(a).

[79.14] See *Tax-Exempt Organizations* § 19.22(b).

[79.15] *Id.*, Chapter 17.

[79.16] *Id.*, § 19.12.

[79.17] *Id.*, § 19.1.

[79.18] These data are presented in the preamble to proposed regulations (see *infra* note 79.19).

[79.19] REG-122345-18 (June 5, 2020).

[79.20] IRC § 4960(c)(2); Prop. Reg. § 53.4960-1(d)(1).

[79.21] Prop. Reg. § 53.4940-1(d)(2)(i).

[79.22] IRC § 4960(c)(3)(B).

[79.23] IRC § 4940(c)(5)(C)(ii).

The proposed regulations define medical services as the diagnosis, cure, mitigation, treatment, or prevention of disease in humans or animals; services provided for the purpose of affecting any structure or function of the human or animal body; and other services integral to providing these medical services that are directly performed by a licensed medical professional.[79.24] Compensation for teaching or research services does not qualify for the exclusion.[79.25] The phrase *licensed medical professional* is defined to mean an individual who is licensed under state or local law to perform medical services, namely, a doctor, nurse, nurse practitioner, dentist, veterinarian, or other licensed medical professional.[79.26]

The term *related organization* means any person or governmental entity (domestic or foreign) that meets one or more of these tests: the person or governmental entity (1) controls or is controlled by the applicable tax-exempt organization, (2) is controlled by one or more persons who control the exempt organization, (3) is a supported organization[79.27] with respect to the exempt organization, or (4) is a supporting organization[79.28] with respect to the exempt organization.[79.29]

The proposed regulations generally utilize the definition of *control* used in the context of controlling organizations in the unrelated business income setting.[79.30] The proposal also sets forth a rule of control in the context of non-stock organizations, entailing a *more-than-50-percent test*, a *removal power test*, and a *representatives test*.[79.31] There is a control test for brother-sister arrangements.[79.32] Constructive ownership rules[79.33] apply.[79.34]

The proposed regulations capaciously address the matter of the excise tax on excess parachute payments.[79.35] They include definitions relating to this phrase.

A *parachute payment* generally is any payment in the nature of compensation to or for the benefit of a covered employee if the payment is contingent on the employee's separation from employment and the aggregate present value of

---

[79.24] Prop. Reg. § 53.4960-1(g)(1)(i).

[79.25] *Id.*

[79.26] Prop. Reg. § 53.4960-1(g)(2).

[79.27] IRC § 509(f)(3).

[79.28] IRC § 509(a)(3).

[79.29] Prop. Reg. § 53.4960-1(i)(1).

[79.30] IRC § 512(b)(13)(D) (see *Tax-Exempt Organizations* §§ 29.4, 30.6(b), notes 81–83); Prop. Reg. § 53.4960-1(i)(2)(ii)-(iv).

[79.31] Prop. Reg. § 53.4960-1(i)(2)(v).

[79.32] Prop. Reg. § 53.4960-1(i)(2)(vi).

[79.33] IRC § 318.

[79.34] Prop. Reg. § 53.4960-1(i)(2)(vii).

[79.35] Prop. Reg. § 53.4960-1(i)(2)(vii).

the payments in the nature of compensation to or for the benefit of the individual that are contingent on the separation equals or exceeds an amount equal to three times the base amount.[79.36] There are exclusions, such as compensation for medical services.[79.37] An excess parachute payment is an amount equal to the excess of a parachute payment over the portion of the base amount allocated to the payment.[79.38]

The proposed regulations address the requirement of involuntary separation from employment, summarize when a payment is *contingent*,[79.39] provide a *three-times-base-amount test*,[79.40] and rules as to calculation of excess parachute payments[79.41]

An issue is whether for-profit businesses are subject to this excise tax because their executives are volunteers at related exempt organizations. This issue arises out of the way an applicable tax-exempt organization's five highest-compensated employees may be identified.[79.42]

The proposal includes several ways to ameliorate this potential problem. First, the preamble states the obvious point that an individual performing services for an exempt organization solely as a bona fide independent contractor is not an *employee* of the organization. Second, an individual who is a bona fide employee of a related organization, including one that provides services to an exempt organization, is not an employee of the exempt organization.

The proposed regulations include exceptions to the definition of the terms *employee* and *covered employee*, and the rules for identifying the five highest-compensated employees, intended to ensure that certain employees of a related nonexempt entity providing services as employees of an exempt organization are not treated as one of the five highest-compensated employees of the exempt organization—as long as certain conditions are satisfied.

[79.36] IRC § 4960(c)(5)(B); Prop. Reg. § 53.4960-3(a)(1).

[79.37] Prop. Reg. § 53.4960-3(a)(2).

[79.38] Prop. Reg. § 53.4960-3(a)(2).

[79.39] Prop. Reg. § 53.4960-3(d).

[79.40] Prop. Reg. § 53.4960-3(g).

[79.41] Prop. Reg. § 53.4960-3(h)-(l).

[79.42] On the basis of guidance issued by the IRS in advance of these proposed regulations (Notice 2019-9, 2019-4 I.R.B. 403), there is concern that these rules would subject a non-ATEO to the excise tax on the basis of remuneration it pays to an employee who performs limited or temporary services for a related ATEO and who typically receives remuneration only from the non-ATEO. In this scenario, the allocation rules provided in that guidance would allocate the entire excise tax to the non-ATEO. This approach is deemed inappropriate because these individuals are performing services for the ATEO solely as volunteers and that application of the tax would force significant changes to avoid the tax, including possible dissolution of the ATEO or the use of ATEO funds to procure services from individuals with no employment relationship at the related non-ATEO. (These individuals considered *volunteers* are employees under common-law standards.)

These exceptions pertain to the individuals' remuneration and hours of service, in the form of a *limited-hours exception*.[79.43] Thus, the proposed regulations provide that, for purposes of determining an exempt organization's five highest-paid employees for a year, an employee is disregarded if neither the exempt organization nor a related organization pays remuneration for services the individual performed as an employee of the exempt organization or related organization. Also, for such an employee to be disregarded, a limited-hours exception must be satisfied, which includes a cap on services provided to no more than 10 percent of the employee's total hours of service for the exempt organization and related organizations during the applicable year. This second element is deemed met if fewer than 100 hours of annual services are involved.

Further, the proposed regulations provide a *nonexempt funds exception* for employees of controlling taxable organizations that perform more substantial services as an employee of the applicable tax-exempt organization under certain circumstances.[79.44] Under this exception, an employee is disregarded, for purposes of the five-highest-compensated employees rule, if neither the exempt organization, a related exempt organization nor a taxable related organization controlled by the exempt organization pays the employee of the exempt organization any remuneration for services performed for the exempt organization. Additionally, the employee must have provided services primarily to the related taxable organization or other nonexempt organization, other than a taxable subsidiary of the exempt organization, during the applicable year.

The limited hours and nonexempt funds exceptions thus exclude certain employees who may be viewed as volunteers (even though, under law, they are employees) from status as one of an applicable tax-exempt organization's five highest-compensated employees.

Additionally, a *limited-services exception* allows an employee to be disregarded for these purposes where the tax-exempt organization paid less than 10 percent of the employee's total compensation and other requirements are met.[79.45]

Finally, the proposed regulations include rules that a member of a board of directors of a corporation or a trustee of a trust is not an employee of the corporation or trust (in that capacity) and that an officer is an employee of the entity involved, unless the officer performs no services or only minor services and neither receives nor is entitled to receive any remuneration.[79.46]

[79.43]Prop. Reg. § 53.4960-1(d)(2)(ii).
[79.44]Prop. Reg. § 53.4960-1(d)(2)(ii).
[79.45]Prop. Reg. § 53.4960-1(d)(2)(iv).
[79.46]Prop. Reg. § 53.4960-1(e)(2), (3).

These proposed regulations include definitions of various other terms, such as *applicable year,*[79.47] *employee,*[79.48] *employer,*[79.49] *predecessor,*[79.50] and *remuneration.*[79.51]

The proposal provides rules regarding when compensation is paid, the entity that is liable for the excise tax and how that tax is calculated, both as to excess remuneration and excess parachute payments, and the allocation of liability for the tax among related organizations[79.52]

For each tax year, with respect to each covered employee, the taxpayer is liable for tax on the sum of the excess remuneration allocated to the taxpayer with respect to an applicable year and, if the taxpayer is an applicable tax-exempt organization, any excess parachute payment paid by the taxpayer or a predecessor during the tax year.[79.53]

For example, if remuneration paid during a year by more than one employer to a covered employee is taken into account in determining the tax imposed on excess remuneration, the taxpayer is liable for the tax in an amount that bears the same ratio to the total tax as the amount of compensation paid by the taxpayer bears to the total amount of compensation involved.[79.54]

§ 5.4 SALE, EXCHANGE, LEASE, OR FURNISHING OF PROPERTY

p. 150, first complete paragraph. *Convert first sentence into separate paragraph.*

p. 150. *Following new first complete paragraph, insert:*

(a) Sales

p. 150. *Insert as last complete paragraph:*

A transfer of property to a private foundation, by a disqualified person with respect to the foundation, in return for cancellation of the self-dealer's indebtedness to the foundation is regarded by the IRS as a sale of the property by the disqualified person to the foundation and thus an act of self-dealing.[84.1]

p. 152, first heading. *Change heading section reference to* **(a.1).**

[79.47]Prop. Reg. § 53.4960-1(c).
[79.48]Prop. Reg. § 53.4960-1(e).
[79.49]Prop. Reg. § 53.4960-1(f).
[79.50]Prop. Reg. § 53.4960-1(h).
[79.51]Prop. Reg. § 53.4960-2.
[79.52]Prop. Reg. § 53-4960-4.
[79.53]Prop. Reg. § 53.4960-4(a)(1).
[79.54]Prop. Reg. § 53.4960-4(c)(1).
[84.1]Rev. Rul. 81-40, 1981-1 C.B. 508.

(b) Exchanges

p. 152, second paragraph, second sentence. *Delete, including footnote, and insert:*

Similarly, a transfer to a private foundation by a disqualified person of real estate, the fair market value of which equaled the amount of a loan made by the foundation to the disqualified person,[98] is an act of self-dealing.[98.1]

§ 5.5 LOANS AND OTHER EXTENSIONS OF CREDIT

p. 163, last paragraph. *Delete last complete sentence, including footnote.*

p. 163, last paragraph, line 11. *Insert footnote 153 following "sale."*

[153] Reg. § 53.4941(d)-2(c)(1).

p. 164. *Insert following second line:*

The transfer of a disqualified person's obligation by an unrelated party to a private foundation results in self-dealing if the foundation becomes a creditor under the note.[153.1] The IRS ruled that an act of self-dealing would occur if a trustor transferred promissory notes, where various trusts that are disqualified persons with respect to an entity treated as a private foundation are obligors of the notes given to the trustor in exchange for business interests, to the entity, which would become the creditor under the notes.[153.2] The IRS also ruled, however, that the trustor's lifetime irrevocable assignment of the notes to a limited liability company and transfer of nonvoting interests in the LLC to the entity will not constitute self-dealing because the entity will acquire the interests in the LLC by gift.[153.3]

p. 164, first complete paragraph, third line. *Insert footnote 154.1 following period:*

[154.1] Reg. § 53.4941(e)-1(e)(1)(i).

p. 164, note 159. *Delete § 5.14 and insert:*

supra note 154.1.

---

[98] A loan of this nature is also self-dealing (see § 5.5).

[98.1] Rev. Rul. 81-40, 1981-1 C.B. 508.

[153.1] Reg. § 53.4941(d)-2(c)(1).

[153.2] Priv. Ltr. Rul. 201907004.

[153.3] *Id.* The IRS further ruled that this transaction would not constitute indirect self-dealing because the entity was not considered to control the LLC (see § 5.11, note 394).

§ 5.6 PAYMENT OF COMPENSATION

(a) Definition of Personal Services

p. 170. *Insert as first complete paragraph:*

The IRS ruled that payments for services provided by a disqualified person, by means of two disregarded entities,[201.1] to a private foundation to enable it to offer "charitable consulting" services and investment services to the foundation and other charities will not be acts of self-dealing because the payments are sheltered by the personal services exception.[201.2] This ruling stated that these services are necessary to carry out the exempt purposes of the foundation, without any analysis of the point; they may be unrelated businesses.[201.3]

(b) Definition of Compensation

p. 172, note 211. *Insert as second paragraph:*

In a case that should be of interest to private foundations that employ one or more children of the foundation's founders, the court assigned the income paid to such children employed by a public charity to their parents for federal income tax purposes, because the parents exercised "complete dominion and control" over the bank accounts in which the payments were deposited (Ray v. Commissioner, 116 T.C.M. 331, 335 (2018)). The court ruled that a "fundamental principle of income taxation is that income is taxable to the person who earns it" and that the "'true earner' of income is the person or entity who controlled the earning of such income, rather than the person or entity who received the income" (at 335–336).

(c) Definition of *Reasonable*

p. 173, note 217. *Insert following existing text:*

See, in general, *Tax-Exempt Organizations*, Chapter 21.

p. 177, first complete bullet point. *Insert as last sentence:*

Likewise, a court concluded that two executives (related parties) were "absolutely integral" to a company's "successful performance, a performance that included remarkable growth in revenues, assets, and gross profits" during the tax years at issue.[242.1]

§ 5.8 USES OF INCOME OR ASSETS BY DISQUALIFIED PERSONS

p. 188, third paragraph, first line. *Insert before existing text:*

Summary of Law.

[201.1] See *Tax-Exempt Organizations* § 4.1(b).

[201.2] Priv. Ltr. Rul. 201937003.

[201.3] See, e.g., § 11.3(d), (e).

[242.1] H.W. Johnson, Inc. v. Commissioner, 111 T.C.M. 1418, 1414 (2016).

p. 189. *Insert following carryover paragraph, before heading:*

Representative Case. The facts of a court case offer an illustration of this type of securities manipulation for the benefit of disqualified persons.[288.1] At issue in this case, however, was the extent to which the amount of an estate's charitable contribution deduction had to be reduced because of post-death intrafamily manipulations that caused property of considerably lesser value than that originally bequeathed to pass to the private foundation that was established by the decedent.

An individual and family members owned a C corporation (Corporation). This individual was the majority shareholder of the Corporation. She created a trust (Trust), to which her entire estate was willed. She also created a private foundation (Foundation), to which the bulk of her estate, consisting primarily of the Corporation's voting and nonvoting stock, was to be transferred from the Trust. One of her sons was the sole trustee of the Trust and the Foundation. This individual died. An appraisal for purposes of determining the date-of-death fair market value of the decedent's property valued her Corporation stock at about $14 million.

Numerous events occurred after the decedent's death but before the bequeathed property was transferred to the Foundation. Seven months after the death, the Corporation elected S corporation status. The Corporation agreed to redeem all the bequeathed shares from the Trust. The redemption agreement was modified, with the Corporation agreeing to redeem all the voting stock and about two-thirds of the nonvoting shares. In exchange for the redemption, the Trust received short-term and long-term promissory notes. Simultaneous with the redemption, three of the decedent's sons purchased additional shares in the Corporation. The Foundation received contributions of the two notes and the nonredeemed nonvoting shares in the Corporation.

The date-of-death value of the Corporation's voting shares was $1,824 per share; the value of the nonvoting stock was $1,733 per share. The value of the voting shares, for purposes of the redemption and stock purchases, was set at $916 per share; the value of the nonvoting stock was set at $870 per share. The appraisal of the voting stock included discounts for lack of control and lack of marketability. The appraisal of the nonvoting stock included those two discounts, plus another for lack of voting power.

The estate claimed a charitable contribution deduction in excess of $18 million, including the date-of-death valued Corporation stock. By notice of deficiency, the IRS reduced the charitable deduction to reflect the value of the notes and nonvoting stock received by the Foundation (about $6 million), thus increasing the estate tax owed. The IRS argued that the manner in which the appraisals were obtained and the redemption of the decedent's controlling

---

[288.1]Dieringer v. Commissioner, 146 T.C. 117 (2016), *aff'd*, 917 F.3d 1135 (9th Cir. 2019).

interest at a minority interest discount indicated that the sons never intended to effectuate the decedent's testamentary plan.

The court of appeals stated that valuation of a gross estate is typically done as of the date of death. Yet, the court added, there is "no uniform rule for all circumstances."[288.2] Also, "[c]ertain deductions not only permit consideration of post-death events, but require them."[288.3] Quoting from another case, the court stated that the "proper administration of the charitable deduction cannot ignore such differences in the value actually received by the charity."[288.4] "This rule," stated the appellate court, "prohibits crafting an estate plan or will so as to game the system and guarantee a charitable deduction that is larger than the amount actually given to charity."[288.5]

The court found that one of the sons "manipulated the charitable deduction so that the Foundation only received a fraction of the charitable deduction claimed by the [e]state."[288.6] The charitable deduction reduction rule, the court wrote, "extends to situations where the testator would be able to produce an artificially low valuation by manipula[tion], which includes the present situation."[288.7]

It is not known why this case was structured as one concerning the amount of the estate tax charitable deduction rather than one involving indirect self-dealing. Certainly, a compelling case can be made that, under these facts, this is more properly an indirect self-dealing case.[288.8]

(c) For the Benefit of Transactions

p. 190, note 297. *Insert following existing text:*

Thus, the author of an IRS private letter ruling missed the mark in writing that the self-dealing rules do "not apply to any transactions between a private foundation and a person who is not a disqualified person" (Priv. Ltr. Rul. 201745001).

p. 190, note 298. *Insert before final period:*

; Gen. Couns. Mem. 39632.

§ 5.11 INDIRECT SELF-DEALING

pp. 206–212. *Delete all text and footnotes under existing § 5.11 and insert the following:*

[288.2] *Id.*, 917 F.3d at 1142.
[288.3] *Id.* at 1143.
[288.4] *Id.*
[288.5] *Id.* at 1143–1144.
[288.6] *Id.* at 1144.
[288.7] *Id.*
[288.8] See § 5.11(e).

As noted, there are two categories of self-dealing transactions involving private foundations: direct and indirect.[382] The Internal Revenue Code and the tax regulations do not contain a unitary definition of the term *indirect self-dealing*. This is the case inasmuch as the IRS believed (and still does) that it was not "feasible to draft a comprehensive definition [of indirect self-dealing] because of the great variety of possible situations which could be called 'indirect self-dealing.'"[383]

Nonetheless, two types of acts of indirect self-dealing are recognized. One of these types of acts of indirect self-dealing is a transaction between a disqualified person with respect to a private foundation and an entity controlled by the foundation. Another type of indirect self-dealing act is a sale or exchange of property to or with a disqualified person with respect to a private foundation while the property is held by an estate or trust in which the foundation has an interest or vested expectancy. The U.S. Tax Court suggested that "[t]here may exist other ways to engage in self-dealing through organizations that are related to the private foundation."[384]

(a)   Transactions with Controlled Entities

Here is an illustration of the first type of act of indirect self-dealing. Private foundation P owns the controlling interest of the voting stock of corporation X; as a result of this interest, P elects a majority of the board of directors of X. Two of the foundation managers, A and B, who are also directors of X, form corporation Y for the purpose of building and managing a country club. A and B receive 40 percent of Y's stock, making Y a disqualified person with respect to P.[385] In order to finance construction and operation of the country club, Y

---

[382]See § 5.3, first sentence.

[383]Gen. Couns. Mem. 39445, which references a memorandum dated December 5, 1972, from then-Commissioner of Internal Revenue Johnnie M. Walters to the Assistant Secretary for Tax Policy (T.D. 7270, LR-1611). The IRS observed that "[t]ransactions between a disqualified person and an organization not controlled by the private foundation are not indirect acts of self-dealing *in most cases*" (emphasis added) and that the Code and tax regulations "do not systematically define all manner of 'indirect' self-dealing; instead, the facts and circumstances must be considered in each case" (Tech. Adv. Mem. 200727019). On another occasion, the IRS wrote that a trust's dealings with respect to a private foundation's "interest or expectancy *could* [not would] result in indirect self-dealing if the 'estate administration' exception to indirect self-dealing . . . is not met" (emphasis added), perhaps suggesting there may be some other exception to indirect self-dealing (Priv. Ltr. Rul. 201849009). In any event, it is the position of the IRS that the concept of indirect self-dealing is to be broadly construed (e.g., Priv. Ltr. Rul. 8942054).

[384]Moody v. Commissioner, 69 T.C.M. 2517, 2529 (1995). The court in *Moody* applied the control test in the regulations (see text *infra* accompanied by notes 392–394) and concluded that the private foundation involved did not control a company under the facts of the case.

[385]See § 4.5.

receives a loan from X. The making of the loan by X to Y constitutes an indirect act of self-dealing.[386]

The first self-dealing case, concerning the private foundation rules, to be decided by a court involved acts of indirect self-dealing.[387] An individual wholly owned corporation A; the corporation transferred two encumbered properties to corporation B, which was a wholly owned subsidiary of private foundation P, of which this individual was a trustee. The individual was a foundation manager of P and thus a disqualified person with respect to P.[388] Corporation A was also a disqualified person because the individual owned more than 35 percent of the total combined voting power in the corporation.[389] The court held that sale of one of these properties by corporation A to corporation B constituted an act of indirect self-dealing.[390] (Transfer of the other property was deemed not an act of self-dealing because, as to that property, A was acting merely as a nominee for B.) Another act of self-dealing was found by reason of the fact that, even though the properties conveyed were encumbered, B paid the full purchase price for them, with the understanding that either the individual or A would satisfy the outstanding mortgage on the properties; the court held that the failure by A to immediately satisfy the liabilities on receipt of the funds from B gave rise to an implied loan to A from foundation P in the amount of the outstanding mortgage liabilities.[391]

(b) Concept of *Control*

For purposes of the rules concerning indirect self-dealing, an organization is *controlled* by a private foundation if the foundation or one or more of its foundation managers may, by aggregating their votes or positions of authority, require the organization to engage in a transaction which, if engaged in with the private foundation, would constitute self-dealing.[392] Additionally, an organization is considered controlled by a private foundation in the case of what would be a self-dealing transaction between the organization and a disqualified person if the person, together with one or more persons who are disqualified persons by reason of the person's relationship with the disqualified person, may, by aggregating their votes or positions of authority with that of the foundation, require

---

[386] Reg. § 53.4941(d)-1(b)(8), Example (1). See § 5.5.
[387] Adams v. Commissioner, 70 T.C. 373 (1978), *aff'd* (unpublished opinion), 688 F.2d 813 (Table) (2d Cir. 1982).
[388] See § 4.2.
[389] See § 4.5.
[390] See § 5.4.
[391] See § 5.5.
[392] Reg. § 53.4941(d)-1(b)(5).

the foundation to engage in such a transaction.[393] An organization is considered controlled by a private foundation, or by a foundation and disqualified persons, if the persons are in fact able to control the organization (even if their aggregate voting power is less than 50 percent of the total voting power of the organization's governing body) or if one or more of the persons has the right to exercise veto power over the actions of the organization that are relevant to any potential acts of self-dealing.[394]

In a case in which a private foundation owned 35 percent of the voting stock of a corporation and a foundation manager owned the remaining 65 percent of the stock but did not hold a position of authority in the corporation by virtue of being a foundation manager, the IRS ruled that the foundation did not control the corporation for self-dealing purposes because it did not have the right to exercise veto control over the actions of the corporation and had no authority over the corporation's actions (other than that represented by its stock ownership).[395] The phrase *combined voting power* includes the voting power represented by holdings of voting stock, actual or constructive, but does not include voting rights held only as a director or trustee.[396]

In a court case, an individual, a trustee of a private foundation and a director of a for-profit corporation, incurred a large bill at a hotel owned by the corporation, which was 50 percent owned by the foundation (permissible at the time[397]) and 50 percent by a family trust. The foundation was billed for these expenses; the foundation refused to reimburse the individual for the expenses because there was no business purpose for them. Following the filing of bankruptcy by this individual, the hotel unsuccessfully sought, as part of the bankruptcy proceedings, to collect its bill from the foundation. The court concluded that the foundation or its managers acting in that capacity did not control the corporation, reasoning that (1) 50 percent ownership is ordinarily insufficient to constitute control; (2) this individual, together with others who

---

[393]*Id.*

[394]*Id.* In one instance, a trust (considered a private foundation) and its trustee (acting only in that capacity) were ruled to not have sufficient votes or positions of authority to cause a limited liability company to engage in a transaction, and a power associated with nonvoting interests in the LLC as a necessary party to vote on the liquidation of the LLC was not considered equivalent to a veto power because the power could not be exercised over an action relevant to any potential act of self-dealing, so that the trust was ruled to not control the LLC within the meaning of the self-dealing rules (Priv. Ltr. Rul. 201907004).

[395]Rev. Rul. 76-158, 1976-1 C.B. 354. In a somewhat similar situation, the IRS did not consider the holder of a power associated with the nonvoting interest in a company, to be a necessary party to vote on the company's liquidation, to be the equivalent of a veto power "in that the other attributes of that interest lack any other powers with respect to operation and management" (Priv. Ltr. Rul. 201407021).

[396]Reg. § 53.4946-1(a)(5).

[397]See § 7.1.

were disqualified persons by virtue of their relationship to him (there were none), could not require the corporation to engage in self-dealing only by aggregating their influence with that of the foundation; (3) this individual lacked actual control, or veto power, over the activities of the corporation; and (4) the corporation exercised considerable independence from the individual and the foundation in seeking payment from them.[398]

The controlled organization may be any type of tax-exempt organization, such as a school, hospital, private foundation, social welfare organization, business league, or (as illustrated above) a social club. It may also be a for-profit organization.[399]

(c) Transactions and the Control Element

The IRS ruled that loans to an entity, owned 34 percent by a private foundation and 50 percent by a split-interest trust,[400] from a publicly traded company, which was a disqualified person with respect to the foundation, were not acts of indirect self-dealing because the foundation held a minority interest in the company, there were no persons who were disqualified persons by reason of an ownership relationship to the company, the trust controlled the entity without the assistance of the foundation, and the foundation did not have any veto power in connection with the company.[401]

The IRS considered the facts surrounding two proposed stock redemptions, where a private foundation would be the seller, and concluded that the foundation and/or its founder did not control the company by virtue of stock ownership or any influence over some of the company's directors, and thus that the redemptions would not be indirect self-dealing transactions.[402]

An individual who was a disqualified person with respect to a private foundation made an interest-free loan to a tax-exempt school to enable the school to complete construction, purchase furniture and other items, and hire staff; this individual also was president of the school. The private foundation planned to make a grant to the school with the understanding that the school would use the funds to repay the loan. The IRS ruled that indirect self-dealing would not occur, because the school was not controlled by the private foundation or the disqualified person. The IRS also ruled that even if the school was controlled by the foundation, there would not be indirect self-dealing in that the grant funds were not "earmarked" for the use or benefit of a disqualified person, inasmuch as the school had "ultimate control" of the grant funds and would

---

[398]Moody v. Commissioner, 69 T.C.M. 2517 (1995).
[399]Reg. § 53.4941(d)-1(b)(5).
[400]See § 3.8.
[401]Tech. Adv. Mem. 200727019.
[402]Priv. Ltr. Rul. 200750020.

"not be bound to use any of the contributed [granted] funds for repayment of the loan."[403]

In a similar circumstance, a grant by a private foundation to a public charity to construct and operate a performing arts center was ruled to not entail indirect self-dealing, notwithstanding the fact that the underlying land was to be purchased from a disqualified person with respect to the foundation, in the absence of any earmarking of grant funds for the land purchase.[404] The grant was made to an intermediate entity, namely, a supporting organization[405] that was not controlled by the foundation or its disqualified persons, nor was the supported organization.

The IRS, however, deviated from this line of law, ruling that a grant by a private foundation to a public charity was an indirect act of self-dealing because, relying on a statement by the foundation (that had no binding legal efficacy[406]), the public charity would transfer the grant property to a for-profit company owned by a disqualified person with respect to the foundation, and because this disqualified person also controlled the grantee public charity.[407] In so ruling, the IRS overlooked the facts that it had earlier found the grant to be a qualifying distribution[408] and that the grant was unrestricted, so that the public charity was free to transfer the property as it wished. The IRS, because of the control of the grantee by the disqualified person, concluded that the grantee was merely an "intermediary," with the grant earmarked for the ultimate recipient, namely, the company.[409] This ruling appears to be incorrect, with the control factor trumped by the fact that the grant was unrestricted. If the property involved had value and the public charity transferred it to the for-profit company without adequate compensation, that would be an excess benefit transaction[410] or a private inurement issue;[411] the self-dealing rules, however, would not be implicated.

(d) Exceptions

The term *indirect self-dealing* does not include a transaction between a disqualified person and an organization controlled by a private foundation, if (1) the

---

[403]Priv. Ltr. Rul. 200443045.

[404]Priv. Ltr. Rul. 201642001.

[405]See § 15.7.

[406]Just as the foundation's "understanding" in the situation that is the subject of *supra* note 403 had no legal binding effect.

[407]Priv. Ltr. Rul. 201719004.

[408]See Chapter 6, text accompanied by note 135.

[409]Were that the case, the grant should not have been regarded as a qualifying distribution.

[410]IRC § 4958. See *Tax-Exempt Organizations*, Chapter 21.

[411]See § 5.1.

transaction results from a business relationship that was established before the transaction constituted an act of self-dealing under the federal tax rules, (2) the transaction was at least as favorable to the foundation-controlled organization as an arm's-length transaction with an unrelated person, and (3) either (a) the foundation-controlled organization could have engaged in the transaction with someone other than a disqualified person only at a severe economic hardship to the organization or (b) because of the unique nature of the product or services provided by the foundation-controlled organization, the disqualified person could not have engaged in the transaction with anyone else or could have done so only by incurring severe economic hardship.[412] This type of transaction was magnificently illustrated by the IRS's approval of transactions between a partnership controlled by a private foundation and a company owned by a close companion of a television icon; the foundation wanted the companion, who was compensated by the company, to serve on its governing board and be one of its officers; the IRS ruled that all of the elements of this grandfathering exception were satisfied.[413]

The term *indirect self-dealing* does not include a transaction engaged in by an intermediary organization with a governmental official where the organization is a recipient of a grant from a private foundation if (1) the foundation does not control the organization, (2) the foundation does not earmark use of the grant for any named governmental official, and (3) there does not exist an agreement, oral or written, by which the foundation may cause the selection of the governmental official by the intermediary organization. A grant by a private foundation will not constitute an indirect act of self-dealing even though the foundation has reason to believe that certain governmental officials would derive benefits from the grant, as long as the intermediary organization exercises control, in fact, over the selection process and actually makes the selection completely independently of the private foundation.[414]

A transaction between a private foundation and an organization that is not controlled by the foundation, where those who are disqualified persons with respect to the foundation[415] own less than 35 percent of the voting power of or beneficial interest in the organization, is not an act of indirect self-dealing between the foundation and a person considered to be a disqualified person solely because of the ownership interests of those persons in the organization.[416]

Indirect self-dealing does not include any transaction between a disqualified person and an organization controlled by a private foundation or between

---

[412]Reg. § 53.4941(d)-1(b)(1).
[413]Priv. Ltr. Rul. 201703003.
[414]Reg. § 53.4941(d)-1(b)(2).
[415]That is, are disqualified persons by reason of IRC § 4946(a)(1)(A)–(D). See §§ 4.1–4.4.
[416]Reg. § 53.4941(d)-1(b)(4).

two disqualified persons, where the foundation's assets may be affected by the transaction, if (1) the transaction arises in the normal and customary course of a retail business engaged in with the public; (2) in the case of a transaction between a disqualified person and an organization controlled by a foundation, the transaction is at least as favorable to the organization controlled by the foundation as an arm's-length transaction with an unrelated person; and (3) the total of the amounts involved in the transactions with respect to any one disqualified person in any tax year does not exceed $5,000.[417]

Indirect self-dealing does not include a transaction involving one or more disqualified persons to which a private foundation is not a party, in any case in which the foundation, by reason of certain rules,[418] could itself engage in the transaction. Thus, for example, even if a foundation has control of a corporation, the corporation may pay to a disqualified person (except for a government official[419]) reasonable compensation for personal services.[419.1]

As will be discussed, another exception in this context is the estate administration exception.[419.2]

(e) Representative Case (Reprise)

As discussed, the issue in a court case was the amount of an estate's charitable contribution deduction, not any aspects of the self-dealing rules.[419.3] The theme of that decision was the manipulations of property, following the death of the substantial contributors, by disqualified persons, destined for a private foundation and efforts of these disqualified persons to lower the value of the property ultimately received by the private foundation.[419.4] The case should have been prosecuted as an indirect self-dealing case.

A set of commentators has asserted that this case was wrongly decided, in that the estate tax charitable deduction should have been allowed at the estate tax value, and that the case should have been prosecuted as a self-dealing case. Specifically, they wrote that the self-dealing tax "should have been imposed on the corporation and/or the decedent's children who wound up acquiring the stock redeemed at what was essentially a bargain price."[419.5]

---

[417] Reg. § 53.4941(d)-1(b)(6).

[418] IRC § 4941(d)(2).

[419] See § 4.8.

[419.1] Reg. § 53.4941(d)-1(b)(7).

[419.2] See § 5.12.

[419.3] See § 5.8(a), text accompanied by notes 288.1–288.8.

[419.4] The appellate court opinion makes three references to "manipulations" of the value of the foundation's expectancy (Dieringer v. Commissioner, 917 F.3d 1135, 1144–1145 (9th Cir. 2019)). See § 5.8(a), text accompanied by note 286.

[419.5] Fox, Blattmachr, & Gans, "Ninth Circuit Affirms *Dieringer v. Com'r*; Post-Death Redemption of Stock Bequeathed to Private Foundation Reduces Estate Tax Charitable Deduction; A Flawed

These commentators, noting that the estate administration exception[419.6] was not available in the case, wrote: "[A] Section 4941 tax should have been imposed on an indirect act of self-dealing. In fact, the tax might have been assessed not just on the corporation but, because it is apparent the sons essentially were indirectly purchasing the stock redeemed, also on the sons, who were also disqualified persons with respect to the foundation."

These commentators also wrote that the stock redemption in the *Dieringer* case "should have been found to have been an indirect act of self-dealing under Section 4941 which may [should be *would*] have (1) forced the corporation or the family shareholders to reimburse the foundation for the excess of the stock's fair market value over the redemption price, which was determined using discounts that do not appear to be appropriate and (2) resulted in excise tax imposed by the section."

(f) Fraudulent Investment Schemes

Private foundations' investments in Ponzi and other fraudulent investment schemes[419.7] raised several issues in the federal tax law context.[419.8] A report by the New York State Bar Association, submitted to the federal government,[419.9] explored these issues. This report concluded that there are no self-dealing issues "that are unique to Ponzi schemes."

The report posited a situation in which a private foundation and a disqualified person with respect to the foundation invested in a Ponzi scheme; the disqualified person thereafter withdrew from the scheme. In considering whether an indirect act of self-dealing occurred, the report concluded that, if the disqualified person was a qualified investor,[419.10] "no act of self-dealing should arise in this situation."[419.11]

The IRS, from time to time, issues private letter rulings as to whether a transaction or arrangement constitutes an indirect act of self-dealing.[419.12]

§ 5.12 PROPERTY HELD BY FIDUCIARIES

pp. 212–215. Delete all text and footnotes under existing § 5.12, other than page 216, and insert the following:

Result Because Taxpayer Apparently Spared Section 4941 Self-Dealing Penalty," Steve Leimberg's Charitable Planning Email Newsletter Archive Message # 281 (April 23, 2019).

[419.6]See § 5.12.

[419.7]See § 8.4.

[419.8]See §§ 6.3(g); 8.4; 9.9, text accompanied by notes 324, 325; 10.3(j).

[419.9]See § 8.4(b).

[419.10]Rev. Proc. 2009-20, 2009-1 C.B. 749. See § 8.4, text accompanied by note 90.

[419.11]The report cited, as authority for this conclusion, Reg. § 53.4941(d)-1(b)(4). See text accompanied by *supra* note 416.

[419.12]E.g., Priv. Ltr. Rul. 200620030.

Property bequeathed or devised to a private foundation is likely to be held, for a period of time before the foundation takes direct title to it, in an estate or trust. While the property is in the estate or trust, the foundation has an *expectancy* or other *interest* in the property. Property of this nature may not be suitable to be held by the foundation, such as property with a lack of marketability. From an economic or business standpoint, the preferable course of action may be sale of the property to another beneficiary of the decedent involved. That approach, however, may be an act of self-dealing. The tax regulations provide some degree of leeway in allowing the estate or trust to sell the property to disqualified persons.

(a) Concept of the *Expectancy*

The federal tax regulations do not address the question of when a private foundation has an interest or expectancy in property held by an estate or trust. These regulations merely make reference to a "private foundation's interest or expectancy in property held by an estate" or trust.[420] Generally, where a charitable beneficiary has an interest or expectancy in property in an estate, the interest is in the residue. This is because the residue consists of funds or other property remaining in the estate after payment of all proper expenses, including taxes, paid in accordance with the settlor's direction.

An aspect of the concept of an expectancy is found in the tax regulations pertaining to the excess business holdings rules,[421] where it is stated that an interest actually or constructively owned by an estate or trust is deemed constructively owned, in the case of an estate, by its beneficiaries, or, in the case of a trust, its remainder beneficiaries.[422] Property that is destined for a private foundation, where the interest has vested, is an expectancy.

Three IRS private letter rulings illustrate the concept of an expectancy held by a private foundation. In the facts of one of these private letter rulings, a trust was required to pay over to the executor or administrator of an estate such amounts as were deemed necessary for the payment of all estate, gift, personal property, inheritance, succession, death, and income taxes, payable by the executor or administrator, or by any beneficiary by reason of succession to the property of the decedent (other than the private foundation involved), and to pay all debts and administrative expenses of the estate and cash bequests under the decedent's will. The trust provided that "all such amounts shall be paid from the portion of the trust estate which passes to [the foundation] under" the trust agreement. This ruling explained the concept of the residue: "That portion of the trust estate, allocated for the payment of these taxes on non-charitable

---

[420]Reg. § 53.4941(d)-1(b)(3).
[421]See Chapter 7.
[422]Reg. § 53.4943-8(b)(1). Also see § 6.2(b).

bequests or transfers, never becomes part of the residuary estate to be distributed to [the private foundation involved] because the residue consists only of funds left in the trust after the payment of all proper expenses, including taxes, paid pursuant to the settlor's discretion." The IRS concluded that, "accordingly, [the private foundation] would have no expectancy or interest in that portion of the assets of the estate."[423]

In the second of these rulings, the decedent's will and trust agreement contained language that was construed by the trustee to require payment of estate taxes prior to calculating the share destined for the charitable beneficiary. The charitable organization involved intended to petition the probate court to determine the appropriate construction of the will. The IRS ruled that the payment of estate taxes in accordance with the findings of the probate court is not an act of self-dealing, even though a private foundation was the residuary beneficiary, because the payment of taxes is nothing more than the payment of a claim against the estate and does not involve a transfer of the foundation's expectancy.[424]

In the third of these rulings, the decedent's will and codicils contained ambiguous language regarding the apportionment of GST taxes. The estate obtained a court order that the GST taxes were to be paid from the residuary interest. The estate's payment of GST taxes from the residuary, in accordance with the court order, was found by the IRS to not be self-dealing, notwithstanding a private foundation as the residuary beneficiary, because the payment was authorized by the will. The IRS ruled that, because the court found that the residuary interest was liable for payment of the GST tax, payment of the tax would not constitute self-dealing because the foundation's interest or expectancy was subject to the GST tax obligation.[425]

(b) General Rules

A form of indirect self-dealing transaction arises where a private foundation is a residuary beneficiary of a decedent's estate or trust: transactions that occur during the course of administration of the estate or trust with one or more disqualified persons can constitute indirect self-dealing.[426]

In the principal case on point, a disqualified person with respect to a charitable trust purchased property from the estate of the decedent who

---

[423]Priv. Ltr. Rul. 9307025.

[424]Priv. Ltr. Rul. 9246028.

[425]Priv. Ltr. Rul. 200225037. Still another example of a private foundation's expectancy is in Priv. Ltr. Rul. 201849009. By contrast, the IRS observed that the "mere possibility that a private foundation will eventually receive property through an estate is not sufficient to make transactions involving that property subject to the self-dealing rules" (Priv. Ltr. Rul. 9222057).

[426]Reg. § 53.4941(d)-1(b)(3).

created the trust. The property was destined to be a substantial part of the trust corpus. The IRS concluded that the purchase was an act of self-dealing because the disqualified person did not pay the estate an amount equal to the fair market value of the property. The matter was litigated, with the trial court and the court of appeals agreeing with the IRS.[427] Another court stated that it is "clear that transactions affecting the assets of an estate generally are treated as also affecting the assets of any private foundation which, as a beneficiary of the estate, has an expectancy interest in the assets of the estate."[428]

(c) Estate Administration Exception

A major exception to the foregoing general rule, provided by tax regulation, is the *estate administration exception*.[429] Pursuant to this exception, the term *indirect self-dealing* does not include a transaction with respect to a private foundation's interest or expectancy in property, whether or not encumbered, held by an estate or trust, regardless of when title to the property vests under local law, if (1) the administrator or executor of an estate or trustee of a trust (a) possesses a power of sale with respect to the property, (b) has the power to reallocate the property to another beneficiary, or (c) is required to sell the property under the terms of an option subject to which the property was acquired by the estate or trust; (2) the transaction is approved by the probate court having jurisdiction over the estate or by another court having jurisdiction over the estate or trust or over the private foundation involved; (3) the transaction occurs before the estate is considered terminated for federal income tax purposes or, in the case of a revocable trust, before it is considered subject to the nonexempt charitable trust rules[430] or the split-interest trust rules;[431] (4) the estate or trust receives an amount that equals or exceeds the fair market value of the foundation's interest or expectancy in the property at the time of the transaction, taking into account the terms of any option subject to which the property was acquired by the estate or trust; and the transaction (a) results in the foundation receiving an interest or expectancy at least as liquid as the one it gave up, (b) results in the foundation receiving an asset related to the active carrying out of its exempt purposes, or (c) is required under the terms of any option that is binding on the estate or

---

[427]Rockefeller v. United States, 572 F. Supp. 9 (E.D. Ark.), *aff'd*, 718 F.2d 290 (8th Cir. 1983), *cert. den.*, 466 U.S. 962 (1984).

[428]Estate of Reis v. Commissioner, 87 T.C. 1016, 1022 (1986).

[429]Reg. § 53.4941(d)-1(b)(3).

[430]See § 3.7.

[431]See § 3.8.

trust.[432] This exception is confined to sales or other dispositions of property by an estate or trust.[433]

The IRS provided a private foundation with a virtual roadmap as to compliance with the estate administration exception. The foundation has an expectancy in the form of shares of stock in a corporation formed by two disqualified persons with respect to it. A court with jurisdiction over the foundation is to determine the "fair value" of the shares, in connection with sale of them to the company, as of a date the court deems appropriate. This court "may determine the fair value of [the shares] to be less than the fair market value of" them. The foundation was required to represent to the IRS its understanding that the estate administration exception will be inapplicable if the court does not approve the sales transaction and/or if an amount that equals or exceeds the fair market value of the shares at the time of the transaction is not received. In essence, the IRS ruled that if the elements of the exception are satisfied, sale of the shares to the corporation will not constitute indirect self-dealing.[434]

The estate administration exception is the subject of several other IRS private letter rulings. In one instance, a private foundation was being liquidated into two new private foundations as part of a plan to settle litigation between two feuding siblings.[435] The settlement plan included reorganization of corporations, some of the stock of which was in an estate and destined for (i.e., was an expectancy of) the foundation. Because the executors of the estate (the siblings) possessed the power of sale, the probate court involved approved the transactions, the foundation was to receive liquid assets in excess of the value of the property it was giving up, and the transactions were to occur before the estate

---

[432]The word *option* is not defined in the private foundation statutory law context. Elsewhere in the Internal Revenue Code, the term *option* is defined to include the "right to subscribe to or purchase any security" (IRC § 1236(e)). The term is used in another Code section (IRC § 2703) but is not defined. Tax regulations in another setting state that the word means the "right or privilege of an individual to purchase stock from a corporation by virtue of an offer of the corporation continuing for a stated period of time, whether or not irrevocable, to sell such stock at a [determined] price … , such individual being under no obligation to purchase" (Reg. § 1.421-1(a)(1)). An arrangement to acquire stock qualifies as an option only where the optionee has the right to obtain the stock "at his election" (Rev. Rul. 89-64, 1989-1 C.B. 91, clarifying Rev. Rul. 68-601, 1968-2 C.B. 204, which states that an arrangement constitutes an option where the stock may be acquired at the election of the optionee and "there exists no contingencies with respect to such election"). As to contingencies, *see* Tech. Adv. Mem. 8106008.

[433]As noted, in the *Rockefeller* case (*supra* note 427), self-dealing was found because the disqualified person did not pay fair market value for the property involved; the estate administration exception thus was not available. The court in that case also ruled that the estate administration exception regulation is constitutional. In the *Reis* case (*supra* note 428), the exception was utilized.

[434]Priv. Ltr. Rul. 201850012.

[435]See § 13.7.

was considered terminated for federal tax purposes, the IRS ruled that the estate administration exception was applicable.[435.1] Thus, despite considerable benefits to the disqualified persons (the siblings)—which somewhat troubled the IRS—the transactions were not considered self-dealing. In a similar situation, the IRS ruled that this exception was available in connection with a series of transactions, pursuant to settlement of litigation, involving a reallocation of assets destined for a private foundation and disqualified persons with respect to it.[435.2]

One IRS ruling involved the division of properties owned by an artist's estate in order to fund a statutory one-third life estate in favor of his wife. The IRS found that self-dealing did not occur, despite the exchanges of property inherent in the settlement, where the agreement satisfied the elements of the estate administration exception.[435.3] In another instance, a business corporation operated to produce and promote a musician's work during his life was bequeathed to private foundations formed to perpetuate the musician's name and compositions. The gift was accompanied by a promissory note because the estate was partially insolvent. The IRS sanctioned this non-pro-rata distribution inasmuch as it was approved by a probate court.[435.4] Likewise, the IRS ruled that a private foundation's holding of a promissory note issued by a disqualified person, and its receipt of note payments from the person after the period of estate administration terminates, will not be acts of self-dealing by reason of the exception.[435.5]

Payments out of an estate's residuary funds made pursuant to settlement of a will contest were ruled to not constitute an act of self-dealing. The decedent had left his residuary estate to a private foundation. The will left nothing to his son but gave the son an option to purchase certain assets from the estate. After controversy surrounding the purchase, a settlement was reached, providing the son part of the assets and placing other assets in a charitable remainder trust for the son's benefit, with the remainder contributed to the foundation. Based on availability of the exception, the IRS ruled that self-dealing did not occur.[435.6] Subsequent rulings indicate that the IRS is often of the view that will

---

[435.1] Priv. Ltr. Rul. 200117042.

[435.2] Priv. Ltr. Rul. 200132037.

[435.3] Priv. Ltr. Rul. 9242042. A substitution of artwork preferred by the artist's daughters, for objects specifically bequeathed to them, however, was ruled to be self-dealing.

[435.4] Priv. Ltr. Rul. 9308045. The IRS also ruled that operation of the business would be functionally related to the purposes of the foundations and thus not result in excess business holdings (see § 7.3).

[435.5] Priv. Ltr. Rul. 201129049. The IRS subsequently adopted a no-rule position as to self-dealing issues involving issuance of a promissory note by a disqualified person during the administration of an estate or trust (currently, Rev. Proc. 2020-3, 2020-1 I.R.B. 131 § 3.01(121)).

[435.6] Priv. Ltr. Rul. 8929087.

settlements are analogous to the circumstances concerning availability of this exception and thus do not entail self-dealing.[435.7]

(d) Determining Fair Market Value

As noted, the fourth element of the estate administration exception requires that the estate or trust involved must receive an amount equaling or exceeding the fair market value of the foundation's interest or expectancy in the property at the time of the transaction.[435.8]

As a general principle, the fair market value of an item of property is the price at which the property would change hands between a willing buyer and a willing seller, neither being under any compulsion to buy or to sell and both having reasonable knowledge of relevant facts.[435.9] All relevant facts and elements of value as of the applicable valuation date must be considered in every case.[435.10] The fair market value of a particular item of property is not to be determined by a forced sale price.[435.11] The IRS observed that "[c]ourt decisions frequently state in addition that the hypothetical buyer and seller are assumed to be able, as well as willing, to trade and to be well-informed about the property and concerning the market for such property."[435.12]

A determination of fair market value is a question of fact; it will depend on the circumstances in each case.[435.13] Valuation of property is "not a precise science."[435.14] The IRS stated that a "sound valuation will be based upon all

---

[435.7]E.g., Priv. Ltr. Rul. 200218036. A court reviewed the constitutionality of the estate administration exception, finding it to be a constitutional tax and not arbitrary and unreasonable (Rockefeller v. United States, 572 F. Supp. 9 (E.D. Ark.), aff'd per curiam, 718 F.2d 290 (8th Cir. 1983), cert. den., 460 U.S. 962 (1984)). The principal contention was that Congress "never intended for [§] 4941 to encompass transactions between estates and disqualified persons" (572 F. Supp. at 13). The trial court seemed to accept that underlying assumption, writing about the "fact" that Congress "failed to mention the word estate in [§] 4941, or related statutes" (id. at 14). The court and the litigants apparently overlooked the reference in the Internal Revenue Code to estates as disqualified persons (IRC § 4946(a)(1)(G)) (see § 4.6). In any event, the court found the regulation to be "reasonable" (id.) and not arbitrary and vague just because it only covers sales and exchanges (id. at 14–15).

[435.8]See text accompanied by supra note 432. The words at the time of the transaction are basically redundant, inasmuch as fair market value is almost always determined at that time. For example, the exception from the self-dealing rules for transactions in connection with corporate reorganizations (§ 5.14, text accompanied by infra notes 460–463) requires receipt by the foundation of at least fair market value, with no reference to determination of the time for establishing that value (Reg. § 53.4941(d)-3(d)(1)), yet surely the valuation date must be contemporaneous.

[435.9]E.g., Reg. §§ 1.170A-1(c)(2), 20.2031-1(b).

[435.10]Reg. § 2031-1(b).

[435.11]Id.

[435.12]Rev. Rul. 59-60, 1959-1 C.B. 237.

[435.13]E.g., Goldstein v. Commissioner, 89 T.C. 535 (1987).

[435.14]Kiva Dunes Conservation, LLC v. Commissioner, 97 T.C.M. 1818, 1821 (2009).

the relevant facts, but the elements of common sense, informed judgment, and reasonableness must enter into the process of weighing those facts and determining their aggregate significance."[435.15]

For example, the IRS stated that the "[v]aluation of securities is, in essence, a prophesy as to the future and must be based on facts available at the required date of appraisal." The agency added that the "prices of stocks which are traded in volume in a free and active market by informed persons best reflect the consensus of the investing public as to what the future holds for the corporations and industries represented." By contrast, "[w]hen a stock is closely held, is traded infrequently, or is traded in an erratic market, some other measure of value must be used." In many instances, the IRS noted, the "next best measure may be found in the prices at which the stocks of companies engaged in the same or similar line of business are selling in a free and open market."[435.16]

The value of stocks is the fair market value per share on the applicable valuation date.[435.17] Where actual sale prices and bona fide bid and asked prices are lacking, the fair market value of a share of stock is to be determined by taking into consideration the company's net worth, prospective earning power and dividend-paying capacity, and other relevant factors.[435.18] Some of these "other relevant factors" are enumerated in the tax regulations.[435.19] The IRS has amplified the factors to be considered in valuing shares of the stock of closely held corporations (or other situations where market quotations are either unavailable or are of such scarcity that they do not reflect the fair market value).[435.20]

These factors, while not all-inclusive, are "fundamental and require careful analysis in each case." The factors are (1) the nature of the business and the history of the enterprise from its inception, (2) the economic outlook in general and the condition and outlook of the specific industry in particular, (3) the book value of the stock and the financial condition of the business, (4) the earning capacity of the company, (5) the company's dividend-paying capacity, (6) whether the enterprise has goodwill or other intangible value, (7) sales of the stock and the size of the block of stock to be valued, and (8) the market price of stocks of corporations engaged in the same or similar line of business having their stocks actively traded in a free and open market, either on an exchange or over the counter.[435.21]

[435.15] Rev. Rul. 59-60, 1959-1 C.B. 237.
[435.16] *Id.*
[435.17] E.g., Reg. § 20.2031-2(a).
[435.18] E.g., Reg. § 20.2031-2(f)(2).
[435.19] Reg. § 20.2031-2(f).
[435.20] Rev. Rul. 59-60, 1959-1 C.B. 237.
[435.21] *Id.*

As the foregoing makes clear, the determination of the value of stock is based on an understanding of all the relevant facts. It is usually prudent for sellers and buyers to retain the services of an independent, competent appraiser, who will ascertain the appropriate business valuation approach and apply the requisite factors in determining the per-share fair market value of the stock involved. Fair market value cannot be ascertained simply pursuant to a negotiation between the parties. That value must be based on the above-referenced standards that have developed in the law. Thus, for compliance with the estate administration exception from the private foundation self-dealing rules, the value of stock and other property must be determined in accordance with the foregoing principles articulated by the Department of the Treasury, the IRS, and courts.[435.22]

§ 5.14 ADDITIONAL EXCEPTIONS

p. 219. *Insert as second complete paragraph, following heading;*

Additional exceptions to the self-dealing rules are available. The principle exception in this group is the one for certain corporate organizations or reorganizations.

(a) Certain Corporate Organizations or Reorganizations

p. 219, second complete paragraph. *Insert as last sentence:*

As another illustration, the fact that the redemption offer by a company was limited to a fixed dollar amount and the fact that a redemption offer by a related company was in tandem with the other offer was ruled by the IRS to not detract from the uniform nature of the second offer.[463.1]

p. 220. *Insert following carryover paragraph:*

(b) Other Exceptions

§ 5.15 ISSUES ONCE SELF-DEALING OCCURS

p. 221, last line. *Delete* are, in reality, *and insert* may be regarded as.

p. 222, note 479, first line. *Delete text following fourth period and insert* See § 1.9(b).

[435.22] Also § 6.3.
[463.1] Priv. Ltr. Rul. 201624001.

(a) Undoing the Transaction

p. 222, second complete paragraph, first sentence. *Delete* **and rescinded (i.e., the property returned) if possible.**

p. 222, second complete paragraph. *Insert as second sentence:*

For example, where a disqualified person sells property to a private foundation for cash, correction may be accomplished by recasting the transaction as a gift by returning the cash to the foundation.[480.1]

p. 222, second complete paragraph, third line. *Insert* **, that constituted the act of self-dealing,** *following* **transaction.**

p. 222, second complete paragraph, fifth line. *Insert* **or persons** *following* **person.**

p. 222, second complete paragraph, last line. *Delete* **deals** *and insert* **arrangements.**

p. 222, second complete paragraph. *Insert as last sentence:*

A correction made in accordance with these rules is not a separate act of self-dealing.[481.1]

p. 222, last line. *Insert* **for cash** *following* **person.**

p. 223. *Delete carryover paragraph, including footnote, and insert:*

of the sale where possible. The amount returned to the disqualified person may not exceed the lesser of the cash received by the private foundation or the fair market value of property received by the private foundation. For these purposes, *fair market value* is the lesser of the fair market value at the time of the self-dealing act or the fair market value at the time of the rescission. In addition to rescission, the disqualified person must pay to the private foundation any net profits the person realized after the original sale with respect to the property the person received from the sale. Thus, for example, the disqualified person must pay to the foundation any income derived by the person from the property the person received from the original sale "to the extent such income during the correction period exceeds the income derived by the foundation during the correction period from the cash which the disqualified person originally paid to the foundation."[482]

[480.1] Reg. § 53.4941(e)-1(c)(1). This is an odd formulation, particularly in tax regulations; this type of transfer is hardly in the nature of a gift, if only because the transaction is not voluntary and there is no donative intent (see *Charitable Giving* § 3.1(a)).

[481.1] Reg. § 53.4941(e)-1(c)(1).

[482] Reg. § 53.4941(e)-1(c)(2)(i).

If, however, prior to the end of the correction period, the disqualified person sells the property in an arm's-length transaction to a bona fide purchaser (e.g., who is not the purchaser or another disqualified person), rescission is not required. In this circumstance, the disqualified person must pay to the foundation the excess (if any) of the greater of the fair market value of the property on the date on which correction of the act of self-dealing occurs or the amount realized by the disqualified person from the sale over the amount that would have been returned to the disqualified person if rescission had been required. In addition, the disqualified person is required to pay to the foundation any net profits the person realized.[482.1]

p. 223. *Delete first two complete paragraphs, including footnote, and insert:*

Sales to the Foundation. In the case of a sale of property to a private foundation by a disqualified person for cash, undoing the transaction includes rescission of the sale where possible. The amount received from the disqualified person in accordance with the rescission must be the greater of the cash paid to the disqualified person, the fair market value of the property at the time of the original sale, or the fair market value of the property at the time of rescission. In addition to rescission, the disqualified person must pay to the private foundation any net profits the person realized after the original sale with respect to the consideration the person realized from the sale. Thus, for example, the disqualified person must pay to the foundation any income derived by the person from the cash the person received from the original sale to the extent the income during the correction period exceeds the income derived by the foundation during the correction period from the property that the disqualified person originally transferred to the foundation.[483]

If, however, prior to the end of the correction period, the foundation resells the property in an arm's-length transaction to a bona fide purchaser (not a disqualified person), rescission is not required. In this circumstance, the disqualified person must pay to the foundation the excess (if any) of the amount that would have been received from the disqualified person if rescission had been required over the amount realized by the foundation on resale of the property. In addition, the disqualified person is required to pay to the foundation any net profits the person realized.[483.1]

p. 224, carryover paragraph, last line. *Insert footnote 487.1 following period:*

[487.1] *Id.*

[482.1] Reg. § 53.4941(e)-1(c)(2)(ii).
[483] Reg. § 53.4941(e)-1(c)(3)(i).
[483.1] Reg. § 53.4941(e)-1(c)(3)(ii).

p. 224, second complete paragraph, first and second lines. *Delete* , and therefore subject to penalty,.

p. 224, second complete paragraph, fifth line. *Delete* deferential *and insert* differential.

p. 225, first complete paragraph. *Delete, including footnote, and insert:*

Use of Property by Disqualified Person. In the case of the use by a disqualified person of property owned by a private foundation, undoing the transaction includes terminating the use. In addition, the disqualified person must pay the foundation (1) the excess (if any) of the fair market value of the use of the property over the amount paid by the disqualified person for the use until the termination and (2) the excess (if any) of the amount that would have been paid by the disqualified person for the use of the property on or after the date of termination, for the period the disqualified person would have used the property (without regard to any further extensions or renewals of the period) if the termination had not occurred, over the fair market value of the use for the period.[490]

As to the first of these payment requirements, the fair market value of the use of property is the higher of the rate (that is, fair rental value per period in the case of use of property other than money or fair interest rate in the case of use of money) at the time of the act of self-dealing or the rate at the time of correction of the act of self-dealing. With respect to the second of these requirements, the fair market value of the use of property is the rate at the time of correction.[490.1]

Use of Property by Private Foundation. In the case of the use by a private foundation of property owned by a disqualified person, undoing the transaction includes termination of the use of the property. In addition, the disqualified person must pay the foundation (1) the excess (if any) of the amount paid to the disqualified person for the use until the termination over the fair market value of the use of the property and (2) the excess (if any) of the fair market value of the use of the property, for the period the foundation would have used the property (without regard to any further extensions or renewals of the period) if the termination had not occurred, over the amount that would have been paid to the disqualified person on or after the date of termination for the use for the period.[490.2]

In applying the first of these payment requirements, the fair market value of the use of property is the lesser of the rate at the time of the act of self-dealing or the rate at the time of correction of the act of self-dealing. With respect to the

---

[490]Reg. § 53.4941(e)-1(c)(4)(i).
[490.1]*Id.*
[490.2]Reg. § 53.4941(e)-1(c)(5)(i).

second of these requirements, the fair market value of the use of property is the rate at the time of the correction.[490.3]

(b) Amount Involved

p. 225, fourth complete paragraph, first line. *Delete and insert:*

The excise taxes for entering into a self-dealing transaction are generally based on the.

pp. 225–226. *Delete last paragraph on p. 225 and paragraph carrying over to p. 226, including footnotes, and insert:*

Use of Money or Other Property. Where a self-dealing transaction entails the use of money or other property, the amount involved is the greater of the amount paid for the use or the fair market value of the use for the period for which the money or other property is used.[495]

Thus, if a private foundation lends money to a disqualified person at a below-market interest rate, the amount involved is the difference between the interest rate set in the transaction (and paid) and the amount that was the prevailing fair market value interest rate at the time the loan was established. For example, if this type of loan is structured using a 6 percent interest rate per annum and the fair market value of the use of the money on the date the loan commenced is 10 percent per annum, the amount involved is calculated using the 10 percent interest rate.[496]

In the case of a lease of a building by a private foundation to a disqualified person, the amount involved is the greater of the amount of rent received by the private foundation from the disqualified person or the fair market value of the building for the period the building is used by the disqualified person.[497] For example, if a private foundation leases office space from a disqualified person for $30,000 annually but the fair market value of the space is $25,000 annually, the amount involved is $30,000.[497.1]

p. 226, note 498. *Delete text and insert:*

Reg. § 53.4941(e)-1(b)(2)(i).

pp. 226–227. *Delete last complete paragraph on p. 226 and paragraph that carries over to p. 227, and insert:*

[490.3] *Id.*

[495] Reg § 53.4941(e)-1(b)(2)(ii).

[496] Reg § 53.4941(e)-1(b)(4), Example (2).

[497] Reg. § 53.4941(e)-1(b)(2)(ii).

[497.1] Reg. § 53.4941(e)-1(b)(4), Example (3).

Exceptions Predicated on Fair Market Value. Where a transaction would not have been an act of self-dealing had the private foundation received fair market value,[501] the amount involved is the excess of the fair market value of the property transferred by the private foundation over the amount that the foundation receives, but only if the parties made a good-faith effort to determine fair market value.[502] A good-faith effort to determine fair market value ordinarily is made where (1) the person making the valuation is not a disqualified person with respect to the foundation and is competent to make the valuation and not in a position, whether by stock ownership or otherwise, to derive an economic benefit from the value utilized, and (2) the method utilized in making the valuation is a generally accepted method for valuing comparable property for purposes of arm's-length business transactions where valuation is a significant factor.[502.1]

Thus, for example, if a corporation that is a disqualified person with respect to a private foundation recapitalizes in a transaction that would be exempt from the self-dealing rules[502.2] but for the fact that the foundation receives new stock worth only $95,000 in exchange for the stock that it previously held in the corporation and that has a fair market value of $100,000 at the time of the recapitalization, the amount involved is $5,000, if there had been a good-faith attempt to value the stock.[507.3] Similarly, if an estate enters into a transaction with a disqualified person with respect to a foundation and the transaction would qualify for the estate administration exception[507.4] but for the fact that the estate receives less than fair market value for the property exchanged, the amount involved is the excess of the fair market value of the property the estate transfers to the disqualified person over the money and the fair market value of the property received by the estate.[507.5]

(f) Abatement

p. 231, second complete paragraph, last line. *Insert* initial *following* the.

---

[501]This rule pertains to two exceptions from the self-dealing rules. See §§ 5.12(c), 5.14(a).
[502]Reg. § 53.4941(e)-1(b)(2)(iii).
[502.1]*Id.* See § 5.12(d).
[502.2]See § 5.14(a).
[507.3]Reg. § 53.4941(e)-1(b)(2)(iii).
[507.4]See § 5.12(c).
[507.5]Reg. § 53.4941(e)-1(b)(2)(iii).

CHAPTER SIX

Mandatory Distributions

§ 6.1   DISTRIBUTION REQUIREMENTS—IN GENERAL

p. 236, note 2, third line. *Delete* related *and insert* integrated.

p. 237, first complete paragraph, second line. *Delete* mandatory.

p. 237, first complete paragraph, seventh line. *Delete* The *and insert* A.

§ 6.2   ASSETS USED TO CALCULATE MINIMUM INVESTMENT RETURN

(c)   Exempt Function Assets

p. 243. *Insert as last paragraph:*

In what may be the most controversial private letter ruling on this topic, the IRS ruled that a private operating foundation may exclude the value of a parcel of undeveloped land in computing its minimum investment return, for mandatory payout purposes, because maintenance of the land in its natural state enhances security for the charitable programs of the foundation and thus is being used directly in carrying out the foundation's tax-exempt purposes. This foundation's exempt activities consist of maintenance of a historic residence, a visitor and garden center, cottages, and buildings for administrative offices, collections and archives, operations, security, wetlands, and storage. The undeveloped land is said in the ruling to defend foundation guests and employees in cases where "physical, biological, radiological, chemical, and human threats may avail themselves." The undeveloped land also provides a study site for schools conducting conservation education programs and serves conservation purposes by contributing to sustainable conservation that improves the health of the community's ecosystem.[47.1]

§ 6.5 QUALIFYING DISTRIBUTIONS

(e) Set-Asides

p. 272. *Delete last two lines, including footnote.*

p. 273. *Insert as third complete paragraph:*

In the event a private foundation is involved in litigation and may not distribute income or assets because of a court order, the foundation may seek and obtain a contingent set-aside.[198.1] The amount to be set aside pursuant to this rule must be equal to that portion of the private foundation's distributable amount that is attributable to the income or assets that are held in accordance with a court order and that, but for the court order precluding the distribution of the income or assets, would have been distributed.[198.2] If the litigation encompasses more than one tax year, the foundation may seek additional contingent set-asides.[198.3] In one instance, a private foundation was ensnarled in litigation over a grantmaking issue, desisted from the making of distributions on the advice of legal counsel, and sought one of these set-asides; the foundation was denied its set-aside request because of the absence of a court order.[198.4]

p. 275, note 214. *Insert before period:*

, along with a user fee ($2,000; $2,500 on or after July 1, 2020); Rev. Proc. 2020-5, 2020-1 I.R.B. 241 § 4.02(6)(a)

[47.1]Priv. Ltr. Rul. 201829003.
[198.1]Reg. § 53.4942(a)-3(b)(9).
[198.2]*Id.* E.g., Priv. Ltr. Rul. 200328049.
[198.3]Reg. § 53.4942(a)-3(b)(9).
[198.4]Priv. Ltr. Rul. 201835014.

CHAPTER SEVEN

Excess Business Holdings

§ 7.1 GENERAL RULES

p. 293, first complete paragraph, first line. *Delete* a *and insert* an active.

p. 293, first complete paragraph, second line. *Insert* generally *following* is.

(a) Definition of Business Enterprise

p. 294. *Insert as second complete paragraph:*

A for-profit business may be started, yet not generate any income for an initial period of time. That undertaking would appear to be a business enterprise as of its commencement, inasmuch as it is carried on *for* the production of income. That is, presumably an activity cannot escape classification as a business enterprise during a start-up period in which income is not yet being produced. The tax regulations provide that, if a private foundation holds an interest that is not an interest in a business enterprise, and the interest subsequently becomes an interest in a business enterprise, the interest becomes an interest in a business enterprise at the time of the change in status.[5.1] This rule, however, applies only where the interest is not a business enterprise because it is a passive holding.[5.2]

[5.1] Reg. § 53.4943-10(d)(2)(i).
[5.2] See text accompanied by *infra* note 102.

p. 294. *Insert as last complete paragraph:*

Four exceptions are available from the definition of the term *business enterprise*: a trade or business of which at least 95 percent of the gross income is derived from passive sources,[9.1] a functionally related business,[9.2] a philanthropic business,[9.3] and a program-related investment.[9.4]

Thus, a private foundation, like all tax-exempt organizations, can be viewed as clusters of "businesses," with some (if not nearly all) businesses related to exempt purposes and some (perhaps) unrelated to exempt purposes. A fragmentation rule[9.5] is used to fractionate each business from the cluster, such as in determining whether a business is related or unrelated. The concept of fragmenting any entity into its ascertainable businesses has taken on new meaning and importance with adoption of the so-called "bucketing rule."[9.6]

(b) Passive Income Businesses

p. 295, first paragraph. *Delete first sentence, including footnotes, and insert:*

The term *business enterprise* does not include a trade or business where at least 95 percent of the function's gross income is derived from passive sources.[10]

(d) Percentage Limitations

p. 299, first complete paragraph. *Delete and insert:*

Generally, ownership of a corporation is measured in terms of the extent of a person's holding of voting stock. For excess business holdings purposes, however, there is a correlation between those holdings and the underlying right, if any, to select one or more directors of the corporation involved. That is, the percentage of voting stock held by a person in a corporation is normally determined by reference to the power of stock to vote for the election of directors.[57] Treasury stock and stock that is authorized but not issued are disregarded for these purposes.[57.1]

For example, a private foundation holds 20 percent of the shares of one class of stock in a corporation. That class is entitled to elect three directors.

[9.1] See § 7.1(b).
[9.2] See § 7.3.
[9.3] See § 7.4.
[9.4] See § 8.3.
[9.5] IRC § 513(c); Reg. § 1.513-1(b).
[9.6] See § 11.5(b).
[10] IRC § 4943(d)(3)(B); Reg. § 53.4943-10(c)(1).
[57] Reg. § 53.4943-3(b)(1)(ii).
[57.1] *Id.*

The foundation does not hold any stock in another class of the corporation's stock, which is entitled to elect five directors. The foundation is treated as holding 7.5 percent of the voting stock because the class of stock it holds has 37.5 percent of the voting power. The foundation is able to elect three of eight directors (37.5 percent); 20 percent of 37.5 percent is 7.5 percent.[57.2]

§ 7.2 PERMITTED AND EXCESS HOLDINGS

(c) Constructive Ownership

p. 303, note 85, second line. *Insert* precisely *following* own.

(d) Disposition Periods

p. 304, note 93. *Insert following existing text:*

An illustration of application of this rule is in Priv. Ltr. Rul. 201849009.

p. 304, note 96. *Insert following existing text:*

This matter of a."plan" is not clear. For example, how is such a plan to be evidenced? Can the plan be only among disqualified persons, or is it contemplated that the private foundation involved must be part of it (the latter interpretation seemingly the most reasonable)?

p. 306. *Insert as first two complete paragraphs, before heading:*

A private foundation had been trying to dispose of its interest in a company, received by bequest, for several years. During the initial five-year period, it was unable to sell the interest because it became embroiled in litigation with a developer. The foundation continued to try to sell the interest, pursuant to a plan submitted to the state attorney general. When the litigation is resolved, the foundation will make "diligent" efforts to sell the interest, including retaining a broker with the requisite expertise. The IRS granted the additional five-year extension.[109.1]

In a similar circumstance, a private foundation retained the services of an investment banking firm to help it sell a collection of retail stores and warehouses throughout multiple states. Despite significant marketing efforts, due to the complex nature of the holding company and adverse marketing conditions, it had been unable to sell the properties. It had a plan to sell the properties to an employee-owned group. It had a back-up plan, submitted to the state attorney general, entailing reorganization of the company and selection of other marketing counsel. The IRS granted the additional five-year extension.[109.2]

[57.2] *Id.*

[109.1] Priv. Ltr. Rul. 201636021.

[109.2] Priv. Ltr. Rul. 201329027.

§ 7.3 FUNCTIONALLY RELATED BUSINESSES

p. 308. *Insert as last paragraph:*

Although this situation does not involve a private foundation, it reflects one of the few times the IRS has ruled on the topic of a functional part of an organization's aggregated other activities. This concerned a tax-exempt professional society[126.1] that has as one of its core functions publication of a journal. The journal is published under a contract with a for-profit publishing company. The society has complete responsibility for the editorial content of the journal; the publisher is solely responsible for selling advertising space in the journal. The issue before the IRS was whether the business of publishing commercial advertising was regularly carried on[126.2] by the society. In concluding that the advertising activities of the publisher are not attributable to the society, the IRS found that the publisher is not acting as the society's agent with respect to those activities. The IRS ruled that, "within the larger complex of publishing an exempt organization periodical, advertising activities are considered separately from the activities of producing editorial material," leading the IRS to decide that the commercial advertising was not regularly carried on by the society.[126.3]

[126.1] An IRC § 501(c)(6) organization. See *Tax-Exempt Organizations* § 14.1(e).
[126.2] See § 11.1(d).
[126.3] Tech. Adv. Mem. 201837014.

CHAPTER EIGHT

Jeopardizing Investments

§ 8.2 PRUDENT INVESTMENTS

p. 322, third complete paragraph, fifth line. *Delete* all.

p. 322. *Delete note 35.*

p. 323. *Delete note 42.*

§ 8.3 PROGRAM-RELATED INVESTMENTS

p. 332, note 63. *Delete text following third period.*

p. 335. *Insert as second complete paragraph:*

Another illustration of a program-related investment was provided when the IRS considered a situation involving a private operating foundation with the mission of conducting educational programs assisting underserved and impoverished individuals. The foundation proposed to operate a loan program in furtherance of its charitable and educational purposes, including making loans to service providers who cannot qualify for commercial loans; loans may also be made to intermediaries and for-profit entities. Loans to service providers will involve below-market interest rates or be interest-free; loans to for-profit organizations will have below-market rates. The IRS concluded that this foundation will maintain significant involvement in the active programs in support of which the loans will be made. The IRS noted that the foundation employs full-time experts in education and related areas, and funds consultants who specialize in assisting service providers and intermediaries who will receive training, knowledge-sharing, data collection, and educational materials to facilitate capacity-building. The foundation will be involved in the structuring of loans, oversee operations of partners funded with loans, and otherwise plan "substantive elements" with respect to the loan program. The loans will not have a significant purpose of income production or appreciation of property.[79.1]

[79.1]Priv. Ltr. Rul. 201821005. See § 3.1, text accompanied by note 32.1.

CHAPTER NINE

Taxable Expenditures

§ 9.1 LEGISLATIVE ACTIVITIES

(b) Law Applicable to Private Foundations

p. 351, note 33. *Delete, aff'd,* 717 Fed. Appx. 712 (9th Cir. 2017).

p. 351, carryover paragraph. *Insert as last sentence:*

This decision was affirmed, with the appellate court stating that these communications "distorted the facts presented to the public or omitted supporting facts entirely," adding that "[m]any of the communications also used inflammatory or disparaging terms seemingly directed at producing an emotional response to the messages' content, rather than promoting an objective assessment of issues of public concern."[34.1]

[34.1] Parks Foundation v. Commissioner, 717 Fed. Appx. 712, 713–714 (9th Cir. 2017).

§ 9.2 POLITICAL CAMPAIGN ACTIVITIES

(c) Voter Registration Drives

p. 359, note 87. *Delete text and insert:*

Form 8940, along with a user fee ($2,000; $2,500 on or after July 1, 2020); Rev. Proc. 2020-5, 2020-1 I.R.B. 241)

§ 9.3 GRANTS TO INDIVIDUALS

(a) Grants for Travel, Study, or Other Purposes

p. 361, third paragraph. *Insert as last sentence:*

In connection with a similar program, the recipients, once the sabbatical period has concluded, are required to submit to the grantor detailed expense logs of their use of the grant funds and a "two-page reflection on their experiences."[98.1]

(b) Other Individual Grants

p. 362, second complete paragraph, sixth line. Delete *indeed.*

p. 362, second complete paragraph, seventh line. Delete *also referred to as* and insert *constituting.*

p. 363, second complete paragraph, first line. Insert *and signed into law in early 2002* following 2001.

p. 363, note 107. *Delete text and insert:*

Victims of Terrorism Tax Relief Act of 2001, Pub. L. No. 107-134, 107th Cong., 1st Sess. (2001), enacting (§ 111(a)), *inter alia*, an exclusion from gross income for qualified disaster relief payments (IRC § 139(a)).

p. 364, first complete paragraph. *Delete, including footnotes, and insert:*

The IRS returned to this matter of disaster relief programs provided by charitable organizations when it issued a publication, initially in 2005 and revised at the close of 2014.[112] This publication discusses employer-sponsored assistance programs involving charitable entities aimed at helping employees cope with the consequences of a disaster. The IRS notes that the types of benefits a charitable organization can provide through an employer-sponsored

---

[98.1]Priv. Ltr. Rul. 201945030.

[112]IRS Tax Exempt and Government Entities Division, *Disaster Relief: Providing Assistance Through Charitable Organizations* (Pub. 3833).

assistance program depends on whether the charity is a public charity,[112.1] a donor-advised fund,[112.2] or a private foundation.

At the outset, the IRS observes that these charitable organizations must demonstrate that they serve a public rather than a private interest and assist a charitable class. The agency notes that, in the past, employer-sponsored organizations were considered by it to "enhance employee recruitment and retention, resulting in private benefit to sponsoring employers," and there were "concerns that employers could exercise undue influence over the selection of recipients." It recognizes, however, that after the September 11 attacks, "Congress took the position that employer-sponsored private foundations should be able to provide assistance to employees in certain situations."

Accordingly, under current IRS policy, employer-sponsored private foundations may provide financial assistance to employees or family members affected by a qualified disaster[112.3] as long as certain safeguards are in place to ensure that the assistance is serving charitable purposes rather than the employer's business purposes.[112.4] Thus, the IRS will presume that payments in response to a qualified disaster made by a private foundation to employees or their family members of an employer that is a disqualified person with respect to the foundation are consistent with the foundation's charitable purposes if (1) the class of beneficiaries is "large or indefinite" (that is, is a charitable class), (2) the recipients are selected on the basis of an "objective determination of need," and (3) the selection is made using either an independent selection committee or "adequate substitute procedures" so as to ensure that any benefit to the employer is incidental and tenuous.[112.5] A foundation's selection committee is independent if a majority of the members of the committee consists of persons who are not in a position to exercise substantial influence over the affairs of the employer.

If these requirements are met, the private foundation's payments in response to a qualified disaster are treated as made for charitable purposes. The payments do not result in acts of self-dealing merely because the recipient is an employee, or family member of an employee, of the employer.[112.6] This presumption does not apply to payments that would otherwise constitute

---

[112.1]See Chapter 15.

[112.2]See Chapter 16.

[112.3]IRC § 139.

[112.4]The publication states that employer-sponsored private foundations can only make payments to employees or their family members affected by qualified disasters, not in nonqualified disasters or in emergency hardship situations.

[112.5]See § 5.8(d).

[112.6]These payments are not taxable compensation to the employees (IRC § 139(a)).

self-dealing, such as payments made to or for the benefit of individuals who are trustees, directors, or officers of the private foundation.[112.7]

In this publication, the IRS states that, even if a private foundation fails to meet all of the requirements of this presumption, "other procedures and standards may be considered to constitute adequate substitutes to ensure that any benefit to the employer is incidental and tenuous, where all the facts and circumstances are taken into account." By contrast, even if a foundation satisfies the presumption, the IRS reserves the right to review the facts and circumstances to ensure that any benefit to the employer is merely incidental and tenuous. For example, a program "may not be used to induce employees to follow a course of action sought by the employer or designed to relieve the employer of a legal obligation for employee benefits."

The IRS has issued private letter rulings on this topic. In one of the first, the IRS ruled that a private foundation providing financial assistance to victims or families of victims of a natural disaster, violence, or terrorist acts of war; victims of discrimination, social injustice, or persecution; and artists was making qualifying distributions as long as the assistance was confined to "impoverished individuals with desperate financial needs."[112.8]

In another instance, an emergency assistance program was maintained by a system of healthcare institutions to provide grants and/or loans to current and former employees of the system and their families and those of system affiliates. Beneficiaries of the program were confined to individuals who were needy and suffered economic hardship due to accident, loss, or disaster; the pool of eligible grantees numbered approximately 5,000 individuals. A committee administered the program, which entailed an emergency assistance fund; there was a formal application process, objective criteria, committee review procedure, limits on allowable assistance, and elaborate recordkeeping practices. The IRS ruled that operation of this fund would not adversely affect the tax-exempt status of the institutions in the system, holding that the class of eligible beneficiaries was "sufficiently large and open-ended to constitute a charitable class," observing that support for the fund would be derived only from employee contributions and gifts from the public.[112.9]

The IRS ruled that a financial assistance program was not a charitable undertaking because a substantial portion of the charitable class to be aided consisted of employees of a related for-profit corporation, thus causing unwarranted private benefit and self-dealing involving the private foundation that would be conducting the program.[112.10]

[112.7] In the publication, the IRS extends this rule to members of the selection committee, although they may not be disqualified persons (see Chapter 4).

[112.8] Priv. Ltr. Rul. 200634016.

[112.9] Priv. Ltr. Rul. 200839034.

[112.10] Priv. Ltr. Rul. 200926033.

p. 364, note 111. *Insert following existing text:*

The President of the United States, on March 13, 2020, declared the COVID-19 pandemic to be a national emergency under the Robert T. Stafford Disaster Relief and Emergency Assistance Act, thereby triggering application of the federal tax disaster relief law, enabling employers to private financial assistance to employees and their family members by means of charitable organizations, including private foundations.

p. 372, second complete paragraph. *Delete last three sentences, including footnotes.*

p. 372, note 151. *Delete* 106–118 *and insert* 106–116; *delete* 17.5(d) *and insert* 17.6(d).

(d) Selection Process

p. 368, second paragraph, third line. *Delete* provisions *and insert* elements.

p. 368, second paragraph, first bullet point, last line. *Insert footnote following period:*

[128.1] A private foundation desired to operate a program by which it would provide scholarships to the children and grandchildren of members of an association; the IRS ruled that these grants would be made on an objective and nondiscriminatory basis (Priv. Ltr. Rul. 201919018).

(g) Seeking Approval

p. 377, second paragraph, first sentence. *Delete, including footnote, and insert:*

Advance approval from the IRS of these scholarship procedures must be sought by means of filing an IRS form.[177]

(h) Individual Grant Intermediaries

p. 379, first complete paragraph, penultimate line. *Delete* organization *and insert* agency.

p. 379, first complete paragraph, last line. *Delete* a stipulated procedure *and insert* the general rules concerning investigation of jeopardized grants.

§ 9.5A FUNDING OF EMPLOYEE HARDSHIP PROGRAMS

IRS guidance recognizes that exempt charitable organizations can serve disaster victims and those facing emergency hardship by providing assistance to individuals and businesses.[224.1]

---

[177] Form 8940, along with a user fee ($2,000; $2,500 on or after July 1, 2020); Rev. Proc. 2020-5, 2020-1 I.R.B. 241§§ 4.02(6)(c), (7).

[224.1] IRS Tax Exempt and Government Entities Division, *Disaster Relief: Providing Assistance Through Charitable Organizations* (Pub. 3833 (rev. 2014)). IRC § 139(a) provides for an income

(a) Guidance in General

In this guidance, the IRS observes that these charitable organizations must demonstrate that they serve a public rather than a private interest and assist a charitable class. The agency acknowledges that, in the past, employer-sponsored organizations were considered by it to "enhance employee recruitment and retention, resulting in private benefit to sponsoring employers," and there were "concerns that employers could exercise undue influence over the selection of recipients." It recognizes, however, that after the September 11 attacks, "Congress took the position that employer-sponsored private foundations should be able to provide assistance to employees in certain situations."

According to this publication, charitable organizations may provide assistance to individuals in this regard in the form of funds, services, or goods to ensure that victims have the basic necessities, such as food, clothing, housing (including repairs), transportation, and medical assistance (including psychological counseling). The type of aid that is appropriate is dependent on each individual's needs and resources. The assistance may be for the short term, such as food, clothing, and shelter, but not for the long term if an individual has adequate financial resources. The publication states that individuals who are "financially needy or otherwise distressed are appropriate recipients of charity." Examples given are of individuals who are temporarily in need of food or shelter when stranded, injured, or lost because of a disaster; temporarily unable to be self-sufficient as a result of a sudden and severe personal or family crisis, such as victims of violent crimes or physical abuse; in need of long-term assistance with housing, childcare, or educational expenses because of a disaster; and in need of counseling because of trauma experienced as a result of a disaster or a violent crime.[224.2]

Disaster assistance may be provided to businesses to achieve these charitable purposes: aid individual business owners who are financially needy or otherwise distressed, combat community deterioration,[224.3] and lessen the burdens of government.[224.4] A tax-exempt charitable organization can accomplish a charitable purpose by providing disaster assistance to a business if the assistance is a "reasonable means" of accomplishing a charitable purpose and any

---

tax exclusion for qualified disaster relief payments. The president of the United States, on March 13, 2020, declared the COVID-19 pandemic a national emergency, thereby triggering application of the federal tax disaster relief law in that context.

[224.2] In a summary of the federal tax law concerning international grantmaking by charitable organizations, the IRS suggested that, to be an eligible recipient of financial assistance in the disaster relief context, an individual must be "needy"; the word *distressed* was not used (Chief Couns. Adv. Mem. 200504031).

[224.3] See *Tax-Exempt Organizations* § 7.11.

[224.4] See *id.* § 7.7.

"benefit to a private interest" is incidental to the accomplishment of a charitable purpose.

The IRS guidelines invoke a *needy or distressed* test. They state that, generally, a disaster relief or emergency hardship organization must make a "specific assessment" that a potential recipient of aid is financially or otherwise in need. Individuals do not have to be "totally destitute" to be financially needy, the IRS stated, "they may merely lack the resources to obtain basic necessities." Yet, the IRS continued, "charitable funds cannot be distributed to individuals merely because they are victims of a disaster." Therefore, a charitable organization's decision about how its funds will be distributed must be based on an objective evaluation of the victims' needs at the time the grant is made.

These guidelines state that a charity may provide crisis counseling, rescue services, or emergency aid (such as blankets or hot meals) in the immediate aftermath of a disaster without a showing of financial need. That is, provision of these services to the distressed in the immediate aftermath of a disaster serves a charitable purpose regardless of the financial condition of the recipients. However, the IRS guidelines state that "as time goes on and people are able to call upon their individual resources, it may become increasingly appropriate for charities to conduct individual financial needs assessments." Said the IRS: "While those who may not have the resources to meet basic living needs may be entitled to such assistance, those who do not need continued assistance should not use charitable resources."

The IRS states that an individual who is eligible for assistance because the individual is a victim of a disaster or emergency hardship has "no automatic right" to a charity's funds. For example, a charitable organization that provides disaster or emergency hardship relief does not have to make an individual whole, such as by rebuilding the individual's uninsured home destroyed by a flood or replacing an individual's income after the individual becomes unemployed as the result of a civil disturbance. This "issue," the IRS writes, is "especially relevant when the volume of contributions received in response to appeals exceeds the immediate needs." The IRS states that a charitable organization "is responsible for taking into account the charitable purposes for which it was formed, the public benefit of its activities, and the specific needs and resources of each victim when using its discretion to distribute its funds."

The IRS guidelines address the matter of charitable organizations' documentation obligations. The rule is that a charitable organization in this context must maintain "adequate records" to show that the organization's payments further its charitable purposes and that the victims served are "needy or distressed." Moreover, these charities are required to maintain "appropriate records" to show that they have made distributions to individuals after making "appropriate needs assessments" based on the recipients' financial resources and their physical, mental, and emotional well-being.

The IRS states that this documentation should include a complete description of the assistance provided; the costs associated with provision of the assistance; the purpose for which the aid was given; the charity's objective criteria for disbursement of assistance under each program; how the recipients were selected; the name and address of, and the amount distributed to, each recipient; any relationship between a recipient and directors, officers, and/or key employees of, or substantial contributors to, the charitable organization; and the composition of the selection committee approving the assistance.

With respect to short-term emergency aid, the IRS guidelines recognize that charities providing that type of assistance are only expected to maintain records showing the type of assistance provided; the criteria for disbursing assistance; the date, place, and estimated number of victims assisted; the charitable purpose intended to be accomplished; and the cost of the aid. By contrast, organizations that are distributing longer-term assistance are required to keep the more detailed records.

The IRS guidance differentiates among employer-sponsored programs utilizing public charities, donor-advised funds, and private foundations.

This guidance states that "[b]ecause public charities typically receive broad financial support from the general public," their operations are generally more transparent and are subject to greater public scrutiny. Accordingly, the IRS states, public charities may provide a "broader range of assistance" to employees than can be provided by donor-advised funds or private foundations. The IRS writes that an employer can establish an employer-sponsored public charity to provide assistance programs to respond to any type of disaster or employee emergency hardship situations, as long as the employer involved does not exercise "excessive control" over the charitable organization. Generally, the IRS observes, employees contribute to the public charity, and rank and file employees constitute a "significant portion" of the organization's governing board.

The IRS states that "[t]o ensure the program is not impermissibly serving the related employer," these requirements must be met: (1) the class of beneficiaries must constitute a charitable class, (2) the recipients must be selected on the basis of an "objective determination of need," and (3) the recipients must be selected by an independent selection committee or adequate substitute procedures must be in place to ensure that any benefit to the employer is incidental and tenuous. As to this third requirement, the charity's selection committee is independent if a majority of its members consists of persons who are not in a position to exercise substantial influence over the affairs of the employer.

If these requirements are met, the public charity's payments to the employer-sponsor's employees and their family members in response to a disaster or emergency hardship are presumed to be made for charitable purposes and not to result in taxable compensation to the employees.

As to donor-advised funds,[224.5] the IRS observes that, in general, grants cannot be made from the funds to individuals. The agency notes, however, its recognition of an exception for certain employer-related funds established to benefit employees and their family members who are victims of a qualified disaster.

Specifically, a donor-advised fund can make grants to employees and their family members where (1) the fund serves the single identified purpose of providing relief from one or more qualified disasters; (2) the fund serves a charitable class; (3) recipients of grants are selected on the basis of an objective determination of need; (4) the selection of recipients of grants is made using either an independent selection committee or adequate substitute procedures to ensure that any benefit to the employer is incidental and tenuous;[224.6] (5) no payment is made from the fund to or for the benefit of any trustee, director, or officer of the sponsoring organization, public charity, or member of the fund's selection committee; and (6) the fund maintains adequate records to demonstrate the recipients' need for the disaster assistance provided.

Under current IRS policy, employer-sponsored private foundations may provide financial assistance to employees or family members affected by a qualified disaster as long as certain safeguards are in place to ensure that the assistance is serving charitable purposes, rather than the employer's business purposes.[224.7] Thus, the IRS will presume that payments in response to a qualified disaster made by a private foundation to employees or their family members of an employer that is a disqualified person with respect to the foundation are consistent with the foundation's charitable purposes if (1) the class of beneficiaries is "large or indefinite" (that is, is a charitable class), (2) the recipients are selected on the basis of an "objective determination of need," and (3) the selection is made using either an independent selection committee or "adequate substitute procedures" so as to ensure that any benefit to the employer is incidental and tenuous. A foundation's selection committee is independent if a majority of the members of the committee consists of persons who are not in a position to exercise substantial influence over the affairs of the employer.

If these requirements are met, the private foundation's payments in response to a qualified disaster are treated as made for charitable purposes. The payments do not result in acts of self-dealing merely because the recipient

---

[224.5]See Chapter 16.

[224.6]The selection committee is considered independent if a majority of its members consists of individuals who are not in a position to exercise substantial influence over the employer's affairs.

[224.7]The publication states that employer-sponsored private foundations can only make payments to employees or their family members affected by qualified disasters, not in nonqualified disasters or in emergency hardship situations.

is an employee, or family member of an employee, of the employer. This presumption does not apply to payments that would otherwise constitute self-dealing, such as payments made to or for the benefit of individuals who are trustees, directors, or officers of the private foundation.

In this publication, the IRS states that, even if a private foundation fails to meet all of the requirements of this presumption, "other procedures and standards may be considered to constitute adequate substitutes to ensure that any benefit to the employer is incidental and tenuous, where all the facts and circumstances are taken into account." By contrast, even if a foundation satisfies the presumption, the IRS reserves the right to review the facts and circumstances to ensure that any benefit to the employer is merely incidental and tenuous. For example, a program "may not be used to induce employees to follow a course of action sought by the employer or designed to relieve the employer of a legal obligation for employee benefits."

(b) IRS Private Letter Rulings

The IRS has issued private letter rulings on this topic. In one of the first, the IRS ruled that a private foundation providing financial assistance to victims or families of victims of a natural disaster, violence, or terrorist acts of war; victims of discrimination, social injustice, or persecution; and artists was making qualifying distributions as long as the assistance was confined to "impoverished individuals with desperate financial needs."[224.8]

In another instance, an emergency assistance program was maintained by a system of healthcare institutions to provide grants and/or loans to current and former employees of the system and their families and those of system affiliates. Beneficiaries of the program were confined to individuals who were needy and suffered economic hardship due to accident, loss, or disaster; the pool of eligible grantees numbered approximately 5,000 individuals. A committee administered the program, which entailed an emergency assistance fund; there was a formal application process, objective criteria, committee review procedure, limits on allowable assistance, and elaborate recordkeeping practices. The IRS ruled that operation of this fund would not adversely affect the tax-exempt status of the institutions in the system, holding that the class of eligible beneficiaries was "sufficiently large and open-ended to constitute a charitable class," observing that support for the fund would be derived only from employee contributions and gifts from the public.[224.9]

The IRS ruled that a financial assistance program was not a charitable undertaking because a substantial portion of the charitable class to be aided

---

[224.8] Priv. Ltr. Rul. 200634016.
[224.9] Priv. Ltr. Rul. 200839034.

consisted of employees of a related for-profit corporation, thus causing unwarranted private benefit and self-dealing involving the private foundation that would be conducting the program.[224.10]

§ 9.6 GRANTS TO FOREIGN ORGANIZATIONS

p. 386, last paragraph, first line. *Insert footnote at end of line:*

[232.1]Convention Between the U.S. and Canada With Respect to Taxes on Income and on Capital, signed on September 26, 1980, as amended by protocols, the most recent signed on July 29, 1997.

p. 387, note 234. *Delete text and insert:*

Convention and Protocol Between the Government of the U.S. and the Government of the United Mexican States for the Avoidance of Double Taxation and the Prevention of Fiscal Invasion With Respect to Taxes on Income, effective as of January 1, 1994 (Art. 22).

§ 9.9 SPENDING FOR NONCHARITABLE PURPOSES

p. 405, note 323. *Delete reference to* Underwood *case and subsequent sentence.*

p. 405. *Insert as first complete paragraphs:*

For example, the IRS ruled that a private foundation's grants to improve students' ability to manage their finances and invest for their future financial security are qualifying distributions rather than taxable expenditures.[323.1] The students involved must be high-achieving individuals with financial need residing in counties with less-than-average median household income. In finding that these grants serve a charitable purpose, as opposed to a private one, the IRS primarily relied on a ruling concluding that a fund used by students as an adjunct to their course of instruction to obtain knowledge and experience in security portfolio management contributes to the students' education.[323.2] As another illustration, the IRS ruled that a private foundation's grant to fund a religious journalism project will constitute a qualifying distribution and not be a taxable expenditure.[323.3] The intent of this project is to produce fair, accurate, and objective articles that explain the religious convictions, practices, and dynamics behind news events. In this instance, the pivotal issue was not private benefit but commerciality.[323.4] The IRS ruled that this project is educational in that it will increase understanding of various religions and the role that religion plays in society. The IRS observed that the prospective grantee will rely

---

[224.10]Priv. Ltr. Rul. 200926033.

[323.1]Priv. Ltr. Rul. 201830003.

[323.2]Rev. Rul. 68-16, 1968-1 C.B. 246.

[323.3]Priv. Ltr. Rul. 201851003.

[323.4]See the discussion of the commerciality doctrine in *Tax-Exempt Organizations* § 4.9.

on members of its staff and contributing authors who are experts in the fields of religious news gathering to "ensure that the preparation of the content will conform to non-commercial educational purposes."[323.5]

A court held that the return of monies to an individual by a private foundation that the foundation should not have received and was not entitled to keep is not an "amount paid or incurred" by a private foundation for purposes of these rules.[323.6] Relying on this case, the IRS ruled that payments made by a private foundation to a trust, as to which the foundation is the sole beneficiary, to cover trust claims and expenses, would not be taxable expenditures because the foundation was returning funds to which it was not entitled in the first instance.[323.7] The foundation had requested acceleration of distributions of trust assets to it before the trustees of the trust knew the full extent of potential claims against and liabilities of the trust. The trustees, facing personal liability, were willing to accelerate distributions to the foundation if it indemnified them. The foundation agreed to refund monies to the trustees should any claims or liabilities as to the trust materialize.

p. 408. *Insert following first paragraph, before heading*:

§ 9.10A DISTRIBUTIONS TO GROUP EXEMPTION ORGANIZATIONS

Private foundations, as part of their program of making grants to public charities, may make grants to entities that have their tax-exempt and public charity status established by means of a group exemption. An organization, such as a chapter, that is affiliated with and is subject to the general supervision or control of a central organization, itself often a public charity, may be considered a tax-exempt organization (and a public charity, solely by reason of its relationship with the parent organization). Exempt status acquired in this manner is referred to as tax exemption on a group basis.[343.1]

Generally, private foundations do not seem to have had much difficulty when making grants to public charities encompassed by the group exemption rules, relying on central organizations' enforcement of the affiliation and supervision-or-control requirements. (The IRS assigns the public charity status of the central organization to the subordinate entities.)

[323.5]It is a non sequitur to state that, simply because this organization's writers are "experts" in their field, the content they produce will "conform to . . . noncommercial purposes."

[323.6]Underwood v. United States, 461 F. Supp. 1382 (N.D. Tex. 1978).

[323.7]Priv. Ltr. Rul. 201745001.

[343.1]The group exemption procedures are the subject of Rev. Proc. 80-27, 1980-1 C.B. 677. In general, see *Tax-Exempt Organizations* § 26.11.

This situation may change. The IRS, in mid-2020, issued a proposed revenue procedure setting forth updated group exemption procedures.[343.2] This proposal includes new procedures a central organization will be required to follow to maintain a group exemption. In understatements, the IRS recognized in the preamble accompanying this proposal that the proposal would make "substantial changes" in the existing procedures and "may" impose "additional administrative burden[s]" on central organizations.

The proposal would require that a central organization have at least five subordinate organizations to obtain a group exemption and have at least one subordinate to maintain the group exemption thereafter. A central organization would be able to maintain only one group exemption.

The term *affiliation* is not defined as such. Rather, the concept of affiliation with a central organization would be demonstrated by the entirety of the information required to be submitted by the central organization about its subordinates. This information would consist of (1) information verifying that each subordinate is affiliated with and subject to the central organization's general supervision or control; (2) a representation that all of the subordinates are described in the same paragraph of IRC § 501(c) as the central organization (with a different rule for central organizations that are an instrumentality or an agency of a political subdivision); (3) if the subordinates are or will be described in IRC § 501(c)(3), their public charity status; (4) a representation that none of the subordinates is organized in a foreign country; (5) if the subordinates are or will be described in IRC § 501(c)(3), a representation that none of them is classified as a private foundation or a Type III supporting organization; (6) a summary of the subordinates' purposes and activities, including their revenue and expenditures; (7) a representation that the primary purpose of all the subordinates (other than those described in IRC § 501(c)(3)) is described by the same National Taxonomy of Exempt Entities code; (8) a statement that each subordinate has furnished the requisite written authorization to the central organization; (9) a statement confirming that all subordinates were organized within 27 months of the postmark date of the group exemption letter request (with exceptions); and (10) if applicable, a statement that any subordinates on behalf of which the central organization will file group returns are on the same accounting period as the central organization.

A subordinate organization would be subject to the central organization's *general supervision* if the central organization (1) annually obtains, reviews, and retains information on the subordinate's finances, activities, and compliance with the annual filing requirements and (2) transmits written information, or otherwise educates, the subordinate about the requirements to maintain its tax-exempt status.

[343.2]Notice 2020-36, 2020-21 I.R.B. 840.

A subordinate organization would be subject to the central organization's *control* if (1) the central organization appoints a majority of the subordinate's trustees, directors, or officers, or (2) a majority of the subordinate's trustees, directors, or officers are trustees, directors, or officers of the central organization.

All subordinate organizations initially included in or added to a group exemption would generally have to meet additional requirements. Generally, the revised revenue procedure will apply with respect to group exemption letters requested and issued after its effective date. The revenue procedure will apply to new subordinate organizations. Certain elements of the revenue procedure will not apply to existing subordinates.

Private foundations making grants to entities encompassed by a group exemption, believing them to be public charities, should be more cautious once the new group exemption rules take effect. Central organizations may not be fully adhering to the new affiliation and supervision rules. The proposed rules as to control are particularly onerous (indeed, unrealistic). Thus, a private foundation that does not engage in the requisite due diligence in this regard may find itself making grants to nonexempt organizations or charitable organizations that are not public charities.[343.3] Expenditure responsibility grants[343.4] may be in order.

§ 9.11 EXCISE TAX FOR TAXABLE EXPENDITURES

(b) Paying or Abating the Tax

p. 410, first paragraph. *Insert as fifth sentence:*

Also, this tax was abated, where the foundation failed to obtain the advance approval of procedures, because its subsequently adopted procedures would have been approved if timely requested and grant funds in the interim were not diverted to improper purposes.[356.1]

[343.3]See, e.g., § 9.9.
[343.4]See § 9.7.
[356.1]Priv. Ltr. Rul. 201940013.

CHAPTER TEN

Tax on Investment Income

§ 10.1 RATE OF TAX

p. 417. *Insert as fourth paragraph*:

For tax years beginning after December 20, 2019, this tax is imposed at a single rate of 1.39 percent.[15.1]

§ 10.3 FORMULA FOR TAXABLE INCOME

(b) Capital Gains and Losses

p. 423, last paragraph. *Delete second sentence, including footnote, and insert:*

There are, however, four exemptions to and adjustments in connection with this general rule. Thus, in the case of property held by a private foundation on December 31, 1969, and continuously thereafter to the date of its disposition, the basis for determining gain is deemed to be no less than the fair market value of the property on December 31, 1969.[46] Another exemption is that gain or loss from the disposition of property is not taken into account for this purpose if the gain or loss is taken into account in computing unrelated business income tax.[46.1]

[15.1] This law change was occasioned by enactment of the Taxpayer Certainty and Disaster Tax Relief Act of 2019 § 206; this act is Division Q of the Further Consolidated Appropriations Act, 2020 (Pub. L. No. 116-94).

[46] IRC § 4940(c)(4)(B). This exception is, of course, dated and presumably of little vitality today. Its concept, nonetheless, was reinvigorated when the Department of the Treasury and the IRS announced that the calculation of net investment income for purposes of the tax on college and university endowment income includes a rule that the basis of property for determining this income is set as of December 31, 2017 (Notice 2018-55, 2018-26 I.R.B. 773).

[46.1] IRC § 4940(c)(4)(A). See Chapter 11.

p. 423, last paragraph, sixth line. *Delete* second *and insert* third.

p. 424, third line. *Insert footnote 46.2 following period:*

    [46.2]IRC § 4940(c)(4)(D).

§ 10.5 FOREIGN FOUNDATIONS

p. 438, note 142. *Delete* E.g., Priv. Ltr. Rul. 201808010.

p. 438, second paragraph. *Insert as second sentence:*

In an unusual instance, a foreign private foundation possessed an investment portfolio held in an investment fund in the United States; this foundation secured a ruling from the IRS that, when the fund becomes a disregarded entity, its income and assets will be reported as income and assets of the foundation, with the income exempt from federal income tax, although the foundation will be required to take this income into account in determining its U.S. source gross income subject to this 4 percent excise tax.[142.1]

[142.1]Priv. Ltr. Rul. 201808010.

CHAPTER ELEVEN

Unrelated Business Activity

§ 11.2 EXCEPTIONS

p. 451, note 64. *Delete* 512(b)(3)(A) *and insert* 512(b)(3)(A)(i).

(b) Rents

p. 454, first complete paragraph. *Delete first sentence, including footnote, and insert:*

The exclusion from unrelated business income taxation for rent is not available unless, as noted, rent from personal property leased with real property is incidental in relation to the total rent involved[79] or where more than 50 percent of the total rent received or accrued under the lease is attributable to personal property.[79.1]

p. 454, first bullet point, last line. *Delete* rentals to be treated as taxable unrelated income *and insert* resulting fees to be unrelated business income.

p. 454, note 82. *Delete text and insert:*

Tech. Adv. Mem. 9822006. Also Tech. Adv. Mem. 9853001. This type of fee-for-service income is not rent (Tech. Adv. Mem. 9901002).

---

[79]IRC § 512(b)(3)(A)(ii); Reg. § 1.512(b)-1(c)(2)(ii)(b).
[79.1]IRC § 512(b)(3)(B)(i); Reg. § 1.512(b)-1(c)(2)(iii)(a).

§ 11.3 RULES SPECIFICALLY APPLICABLE TO PRIVATE FOUNDATIONS

(b) Permitted Businesses

p. 462, last paragraph. *Insert as last sentence:*

The law as to functionally related businesses is discussed elsewhere.[133.1]

p. 462, note 131, last line. *Delete text following fourth period.*

p. 469. *Insert following second complete paragraph, before heading:*

(f) Rental Activity

The rules as to rental income, as applicable to private foundations, were nicely illustrated by a situation in which a private foundation had a significant expectancy in the assets of a limited liability company that included an apartment complex. The services provided to tenants of the apartment units are limited to necessary and customary maintenance and utility services. The maintenance staff provides janitorial and related services only for the common areas. Tenants are responsible for paying for their own gas and electric services, and for their share of water, sewer, and garbage services. An independent company provides security services. Apartment units are unfurnished; they contain only the usual kitchen and laundry appliances, as to which separate rent is not charged.[159.1] None of this rent is based in whole or in part on the income or profits derived by any person from the leased property.[159.2] The LLC's real property is subject to a mortgage.[159.3] The IRS ruled that the payments from tenants received by the LLC (and indirectly by the foundation) are rent from real property excludible from unrelated business income, except to the extent attributable to debt-financed property.[159.4]

§ 11.4 UNRELATED DEBT-FINANCED INCOME RULES

(a) Acquisition Indebtedness

p. 470, note 161, last line. *Insert before last period:*

(where the IRS held that, although a private foundation's participation in a rezoning agreement obligated it to reimburse a developer for its portion of rezoning costs and pay the developer

---

[133.1] See § 7.3.

[159.1] The portion of rent attributable to these appliances was said to be minimal (i.e., "well below" 5 percent of the total rent). See text accompanied by *supra* note 79.

[159.2] See text accompanied by *supra* note 80.

[159.3] See § 11.4.

[159.4] Priv. Ltr. Rul. 201849009.

a fee in the event of successful completion of the rezoning, the agreement did not create an unconditional and legally enforceable obligation for payment of a fixed or determinate sum of money, so that the foundation was found to not have incurred indebtedness and thus an acquisition indebtedness did not arise)

p. 470, note 163. *Insert following existing text:*

In connection with a fact situation discussed earlier (text accompanied by *supra* note 81.4), an interest in the LLC was held by a trust formed for the benefit of the trustor's surviving spouse. The IRS observed that the distribution of the trust's interest in the LLC to the foundation after the spouse's death will be a devise from the spouse. Thus, the IRS ruled, any indebtedness secured by mortgages against real property owned by the LLC will not be treated as acquisition indebtedness during a period of 10 years following the date of acquisition by the foundation of any interest in the company, provided that the foundation does not assume and agree to pay the indebtedness secured by the mortgage and does not make any payment for the equity in the property (Priv. Ltr. Rul. 201849009).

p. 470, note 165. *Insert* , e.g., *following* See.

§ 11.5 CALCULATING AND REPORTING THE TAX

(a) General Rules

p. 474, note 193. *Delete* 162 *and insert* 512(a)(1).

(b) Bucketing Rule

p. 475, third complete paragraph, first line. *Insert* Statutory Law. *before existing text.*

p. 476, note 201, third line. *Insert following* computation:

, known as the "bucketing" (or "silo") rule,

p. 476, note 202. *Delete text and insert:*

See text accompanied by *infra* note 214.

p. 476, note 203. *Delete text and insert:*

IRC § 172(b)(1).

Proposed Regulations. The Treasury Department and the IRS, in early 2020, issued proposed regulations concerning the bucketing rule.[203.1] In essence, the bucketing rule is this: An exempt organization with more than one unrelated business must compute UBTI separately with respect to each unrelated business.[203.2] An organization identifies its separate unrelated businesses using the rules that follow.[203.3]

[203.1] REG-106864-18 (April 23, 2020).
[203.2] Prop. Reg. § 1.512(a)-6(a)(1).
[203.3] Prop. Reg. § 1.512(a)-6(a)(2).

The preamble to these proposed regulations states that "[t]here is no general statutory or regulatory definition of what activities constitute" a business for unrelated business purposes.[203.4] In a notice preceding these proposed regulations,[203.5] Treasury and the IRS stated they were considering use of the North American Industry Classification System (NAICS) codes as *a* method for determining whether an exempt organization has more than one unrelated business and for purposes of calculating UBTI. In the proposed regulations, the NAICS codes are *the* system for these purposes, albeit using only the first two digits of the six-digit codes.[203.6] This approach is seen by the government as "administrable" for exempt organizations.[203.7]

These codes are to be reported only once, even though there may be some expansion of the activities. The codes are not to be changed unless it can be shown that the initial code was chosen in error and that another code is more descriptive.

The government does not anticipate the need to change this method. As more experience is gained, Treasury and the IRS "may" consider additional methods for identifying separate businesses and will publish guidance "as needed."

In the notice, Treasury and the IRS expressed concerns with matters of deductions against gross unrelated income from an unrelated business and allocation of indirect expenses between or among unrelated businesses. The government observed that permitting allocation methods based solely on reasonableness is difficult for the IRS to administer and may not provide certainty for taxpayers. This issue remains under consideration and a separate proposal will be issued.[203.8]

The proposed regulations discuss the deductibility of tax return preparation fees and pronounce, as not reasonable, allocation of expenses, depreciation, and similar items using an unadjusted gross-to-gross method.[203.9]

[203.4] The preamble sidestepped acknowledgment of any *judicial* definition of the concept. See text accompanied by *infra* notes 203.35–203.44.

[203.5] Notice 2018-67, 2018-36 I.R.B. 409.

[203.6] Prop. Reg. § 1.512(a)-6(b).

[203.7] These proposed regulations are, in several respects, more favorable, from an exempt organization's standpoint, than the guidance in the notice. Classification of unrelated business activities based on a two-digit NAICS system, rather than one based on six digits, will give exempt organizations greater latitude in combining similar activities into a single business. This topic is, however, a matter of law; thus, there should be substantive policy guidance on the point in the regulations, such as along the lines of the U.S. Tax Court's opinions concerning the conduct of businesses by marijuana dispensaries (see the text accompanied by *infra* notes 203.35–203.44). That type of legal analysis, along with the codes, would be more in keeping with the tenor of the existing regulations and the seriousness of the topic.

[203.8] But see Prop. Reg. § 1.512(a)-1(a), (b).

[203.9] As to the latter, Prop. Reg. § 1.512(a)-1(c).

The proposed regulations generally permit aggregation of specifically listed investment activities for bucketing rule purposes. These activities are not identified using NAICS codes. Thus, an exempt organization's investment activities generally are treated as a separate unrelated business for these purposes.[203.10]

The proposal provides an exclusive list of an exempt organization's investment activities that can be treated as one unrelated business. (In addition, most forms of passive income, such as dividends, interest, annuities, rents, royalties, and capital gains, are excluded from UBI.[203.11]) Generally, these investments are limited to qualifying partnership interests, qualifying S corporation interests, and debt-financed properties (see below).[203.12]

Treasury and the IRS are considering whether the term *investment activities* can be defined more generally and have requested comments regarding the specific factors that may be involved.

The proposed regulations generally retain the rules described in the notice that (1) an exempt organization is permitted to aggregate its UBTI from certain partnership interests with multiple businesses, including businesses conducted by lower-tier partnerships (i.e., *qualifying partnership interests*), and (2) a QPI may be aggregated with other QPIs, resulting in treatment of the group of QPIs as a single unrelated business.[203.13]

There are, however, modifications. One modification is that, once an exempt organization designates a partnership interest as a QPI, it cannot thereafter identify the unrelated businesses conducted by the partnership using NAICS codes unless and until the partnership interest is no longer a QPI.

A partnership interest is a qualifying partnership interest if the exempt organization holds a direct interest in a partnership that meets the requirements of a de minimis test or a control test.[203.14] Pursuant to a look-through rule, if an exempt organization does not control a partnership in which it holds a direct interest, but the partnership interest is not a QPI because the organization holds more than 20 percent of the capital interest (see below), any partnership in which the organization holds an indirect interest through the directly held partnership interest may be a QPI if the indirectly held partnership interest meets the de minimis test.[203.15] In this circumstance, the investment can be aggregated with other de minimis investments.

[203.10]Prop. Reg. § 1.512(a)-6(c)(1).

[203.11]IRC § 512(b)(1)-(3), (5).

[203.12]Prop. Reg. § 1.512(a)-6(c)(1).

[203.13]In general, *Tax-Exempt Organizations* § 24.7.

[203.14]Prop. Reg. § 1.512(a)-6(c)(2)(i).

[203.15]Prop. Reg. § 1.512(a)-6(c)(2)(ii).

A partnership interest is a QPI by reason of the de minimis test if the exempt organization involved directly or indirectly holds no more than 2 percent of the profits interest and no more than 2 percent of the capital interest.[203.16]

If a directly held partnership interest is not a QPI, the exempt organization is required to identify the businesses conducted by the directly held partnership, and any indirectly held partnerships, that are unrelated businesses with respect to the exempt organization.

The notice stated that a partnership interest is a QPI pursuant to the control test if the exempt organization holds no more than 20 percent of the capital interest and does not have control or influence over the partnership. The proposed regulations retain this 20-percent threshold and generally retain the control rule.[203.17] (The word *influence* has been removed.) The proposal provides that all facts and circumstances are relevant for determining whether an exempt organization controls a partnership and lists certain circumstances that evidence control.[203.18]

The notice included with the control test a rule requiring exempt organizations to combine certain related interests. The proposed regulations have a modified aggregation rule to address situations in which an exempt organization may control a partnership by means of a combination of interests (such as by use of a supporting organization[203.19]).[203.20]

The proposed regulations permit reliance on Schedule K-1 (Form 1065), for purposes of measuring an exempt organization's ownership interest in a pass-through entity, if the schedule lists the exempt organization's percentage profits interest or its percentage capital interest, or both, at the beginning and end of the year.[203.21] An exempt organization may not, however, rely on the schedule to the extent any information about the organization's percentage interest is not specifically provided. Treasury and the IRS are considering revisions to the schedule.

The proposed regulations address the treatment of certain deemed unrelated business income. As to unrelated debt-financed income,[203.22] the proposal includes all the UBTI from financed properties in the list of investment activities treated as a separate unrelated business (see above). The proposal permits an exempt organization to aggregate all the specified payments received from a controlled organization[203.23] and treat the payments as received from a single

---

[203.16]Prop. Reg. § 1.512(a)-6(c)(3).

[203.17]Prop. Reg. § 1.512(a)-6(c)(4)(i).

[203.18]Prop. Reg. § 1.512(a)-6(c)(4)(iii).

[203.19]See § 15.7.

[203.20]Prop. Reg. § 1.512(a)-6(c)(4)(ii).

[203.21]Prop. Reg. § 1.512(a)-6(c)(5)(i).

[203.22]See § 11.4.

[203.23]IRC § 512(b)(13). See *Tax-Exempt Organizations* §§ 29.7, 30.6.

unrelated business. It treats the provision of insurance by all controlled foreign corporations[203.24] as one business, regardless of whether the insurance income is received from more than one controlled foreign corporation.[203.25]

The proposal permits an exempt organization to aggregate its UBTI from an interest in an S corporation[203.26] with its UBTI from other investment activities if the exempt organization's stock ownership, by percentage, in the corporation meets the de minimis or control test (see above).[203.27]

The proposed regulations provide that the total UBTI of an exempt organization with more than one unrelated business is the sum of the UBTI computed with respect to each unrelated business, less the specific deduction.[203.28]

Likewise, the charitable contribution deductions[203.29] are to be taken against UBTI.

The proposed regulations state that an exempt organization with more than one unrelated business determines the net operating loss deduction[203.30] separately with respect to each unrelated business.[203.31]

The proposal clarifies that an inclusion of subpart F income[203.32] is treated in the same manner as a dividend. It further clarifies that an inclusion of global intangible low-taxed income[203.33] is treated in the same manner as an inclusion of subpart F income. The IRS will be updating Form 990-T and its schedules and instructions.

Consequently, because private foundations are not likely to have conventional unrelated business activity due to application of the excess business holdings rules,[203.34] the principal aspect of the bucketing rule to them currently appears to be in connection with their investments and involvement in partnerships.

Case Law. Much discussion has ensued, in the aftermath of enactment of the bucketing rule, about the absence of law that tax-exempt organizations may use in ascertaining whether they have more than one unrelated business. Certainly, nothing currently in the statutes or tax regulations addresses the topic. The IRS has, as noted, issued preliminary guidance in this area.

There is case law, nonetheless, that can be of assistance in this context. This body of law has arisen in connection with the federal tax law treatment of the

---

[203.24]IRC § 512(b)(17). See *Tax-Exempt Organizations* § 25.1(n).

[203.25]As to *supra* notes 203.22–203.24, Prop. Reg. § 1.512(a)-6(d)(1).

[203.26]IRC § 512(e). See *Tax-Exempt Organizations* § 25.2(m).

[203.27]Prop. Reg. § 1.512(a)-6(e).

[203.28]IRC § 512(b)(12). See *Tax-Exempt Organizations* § 25.7(c).

[203.29]IRC § 512(b)(10), (11). See *Tax-Exempt Organizations* § 25.7(b).

[203.30]IRC § 512(b)(6). See *Tax-Exempt Organizations* § 25.7(d).

[203.31]Prop. Reg. § 1.512(a)-6(h).

[203.32]IRC § 951(a)(1)(A).

[203.33]IRC § 951A-(a).

[203.34]See Chapter 7.

expenses incurred by marijuana dispensaries. Marijuana, of course, is a controlled substance under federal law, and its manufacture and distribution are thus forbidden at that law level.[203.35] Some states, however, have adopted laws allowing for the cultivation, sale, and use of marijuana for personal medicinal purposes. The tensions between these two bodies of law are manifold, two being that a business that "consists of trafficking in controlled substances" may not deduct (under federal law) any business expenses[203.36] and thus cannot capitalize costs.[203.37] This state of the federal tax law has incentivized these companies to assert that they are operating one or more businesses of a type other than dispensation of marijuana and required courts to rule on that assertion.

As an example, the U.S. Tax Court held that one of these companies operated two separate businesses—one involving the sale of marijuana and one that provides caregiving services.[203.38] This decision enabled the company to deduct the expenses allocable to the caregiving business. In two subsequent cases, the court found that a marijuana dispensary was engaged in a single business.[203.39]

In a case decided near the close of 2018, the Tax Court considered the contention of a company that it is engaging in four discrete businesses: sales of marijuana and products containing it, sales of products without marijuana, therapeutic services, and brand development. The court, however, held that this entity is engaged in merely one business: trafficking in a controlled substance.[203.40] Thus, the company cannot, pursuant to this holding, deduct any of its expenses.[1]

In this 2018 opinion, the Tax Court enunciated principles that are useful in the exempt organizations' unrelated business setting. The court first noted that an "activity is a trade or business if the taxpayer does it continuously and regularly with the intent of making a profit."[203.42] Then, it provided four basic guidelines: (1) an organization can operate more than one business; (2) multiple activities can amount to a single business; (3) whether two activities are two businesses or only one is a question of fact; and (4) the court primarily considers, in ascertaining the number of an organization's businesses, the degree of organizational and economic interrelationship of various undertakings, the business purpose that is (or might be) served by carrying on the various undertakings separately or together, and the similarity of the various undertakings.

[203.35]21 U.S.C. §§ 812, 841(a).

[203.36] IRC § 280E.

[203.37]IRC § 263A(a)(2).

[203.38]Californians Helping to Alleviate Medical Problems, Inc. v. Commissioner, 128 T.C. 173 (2007).

[203.39]Canna Care, Inc. v. Commissioner, 110 T.C.M. 408 (2015), aff'd, 694 Fed. Appx. 570 (9th Cir. 2017); Olive v. Commissioner, 139 T.C. 19 (2012), aff'd, 792 F.3d 1146 (9th Cir. 2015).

[203.40]Patients Mutual Assistance Collective Corp. v. Commissioner, 116 T.C.M. 570 (2018).

[1]Likewise, Richmond Patients Group v. Commissioner, T.C. Memo, 2050-52 (May 4, 2020).

[203.42]*Id.* at ___.

Factors in the cases were elements such as different employees for different functions, substantial differences in services, the bundling of services, the fact that some activities were incidental to others, the income amounts associated with each activity, and use of one entity, management, capital structure, and facilities. In this case, the court noted that the organization's marijuana and marijuana products sales accounted for 99.5 percent of its revenue. Its other activities were "neither economically separate nor substantially different."[203.43]

Thus, while the nonprofit community and the Treasury Department are now struggling to understand and implement the bucketing rule, the U.S. Tax Court has been working on and developing these concepts since 2007.

(b-1) Fringe Benefit Expense Rules

Expenses associated with certain fringe benefit plans operated by tax-exempt organizations are treated as forms of unrelated business income.[203.44] These expenses are those for a qualified transportation fringe,[203.45] a parking facility used in connection with qualified parking,[203.46] or an on-premises athletic facility.[203.47] *Qualified parking* is parking provided to an employee on or near the business premises of the employer or on or near a location from which the employee commutes to work. This body of law was created in an effort to achieve parity between taxable and tax-exempt employers (the former cannot deduct these expenses[203.48]). These rules were, however, retroactively repealed in 2019.[203.49]

(d) Other Tax Computation and Reporting Rules

p. 477, fourth complete paragraph. *Delete, including footnotes, and insert:*

Gross income from an unrelated trade or business must be reported to the IRS, along with associated deductions, on the unrelated business tax return.[213] In reflection of the bucketing rule,[214] an organization with more than one unrelated trade or business should report one of them on the face of

---

[203.43] *Id.* at ___. Likewise, Alternative Health Care Advocates v. Commissioner, 151 T.C. 225 (2018).
[203.44] IRC § 512(a)(7), also added by the Tax Cuts and Jobs Act.
[203.45] IRC § 132(f)(1).
[203.46] IRC § 132(f)(5)(C).
[203.47] IRC § 132(j)(4)(B).
[203.48] IRC § 274.
[203.49] Taxpayer Certainty and Disaster Relief Act of 2019 § 302; this act is Division Q of the Further Consolidated Appropriations Act, 2020 (Pub. L. No. 116-94).
[213] Form 990-T, Parts I, II.
[214] See § 11.5(b).

the return[214.1] and complete and attach a separate filing for each additional trade or business.[214.2]

p. 477, note 214, first line. *Delete text following period.*

pp. 477–478. *Delete last paragraph on p. 477 and text on p. 478, including footnotes.*

[214.1]Form 990-T, Parts I, II.
[214.2]Form 990-T, Schedule M.

CHAPTER TWELVE

Tax Compliance and Administrative Issues

pp. 479–566. *Delete chapter.*

CHAPTER THIRTEEN

Termination of Foundation Status

§ 13.1 VOLUNTARY TERMINATION

p. 570, note 18. *Delete text and insert:*

Form 8940, along with a user fee of $400, which differentiates between terminations involving an advance ruling request and those where the 60-month period has ended (Rev. Proc. 2020-5, 2020-1 I.R.B. 241 § 4.02(6)(h), (i)).

§ 13.3 TRANSFER OF ASSETS TO A PUBLIC CHARITY

(c) Eligible Public Charity Recipients

p. 579, fifth paragraph, second line. *Delete* should *and insert* must.

p. 579, note 63. *Delete text and insert:*

Form 8940, along with a user fee ($400; $500 on or after July 1, 2020); Rev. Proc. 2020-5, 2020-1 I.R.B. 241 § 4.02(6)(h), (i).

§ 13.4 OPERATION AS A PUBLIC CHARITY

p. 580, note 66, second line. *Insert before period:*

(Rev. Proc. 2020-5, 2020-1 I.R.B. 241 § 4.02(6)(h), (i))

§ 13.6 TERMINATION TAX

p. 597. *Insert following first complete paragraph, before heading:*

The IRS ruled that a charitable lead annuity trust will terminate on the designated termination date and that the termination will not give rise to the private foundation termination tax.[160.1] A charitable lead annuity trust was established, with Charity C granted the annuity interest. On expiration of the term of this income interest, the trustee is to distribute the trust principal to the grantor's children. This term is set to be just sufficient to make the income interest in the trust, for which an estate tax charitable deduction would be allowed, have an aggregate value of X percent of the total fair market value of all amounts in the trust as of its commencement. The annuity amount is to be paid in equal quarterly installments. By court order, Charity C was divided into two private foundations, Charity A and Charity B. A and B each received one-half of C's annuity interest in the trust.

The principal issue was whether termination of the trust on the termination date will result in imposition of a termination tax. The IRS noted that the trust is terminating by reason of a payment to a beneficiary that is directed by the terms of the governing instrument of the trust, rather than being discretionary with the trustee.[160.2] The agency stated that when the trust terminates (on the termination date), the law treating the trust as a private foundation will cease to apply because the trust will no longer retain any amounts for which the charitable deduction was allowed. Thus, the IRS ruled, the final payment to the remainder interest beneficiaries will not be considered a termination of the trust's private foundation status. Without the requisite termination, the IRS ruled, a termination tax will not apply to the trust.

[160.1] Priv. Ltr. Rul. 201930017.
[160.2] Reg. § 53.4947-1(e)(1).

CHAPTER FOURTEEN

Charitable Giving Rules

§ 14.1 CONCEPT OF GIFT

p. 600. *Insert as third complete paragraph:*

Thus, as these definitions indicate, a transfer that causes the transferor to receive a substantial quid pro quo in exchange for the amount or value transferred cannot qualify as a gift. This concept of the quid pro quo in the charitable contribution context gained national attention when the Department of the Treasury and the IRS used it to combat the efforts in some states to circumvent the $10,000 limit on the deductibility of state and local taxes[9.1] by substituting an increased charitable deduction for a disallowed state and local tax deduction. Final regulations were issued, providing rules stating the lack of availability of federal income tax charitable contribution deductions when a transfer of money or other property is made pursuant to one of these SALT cap "workarounds."[9.2] The general rule, under this proposal, is that when a taxpayer receives or expects to receive a state or local tax credit in return for a payment to a charitable organization, the receipt of the tax benefit constitutes a quid pro quo that may preclude a full charitable deduction. That is, the amount

---

[9.1] IRC § 164(b)(6). This provision was added to the IRC on enactment of the fiscal year 2018 budget reconciliation legislation (informally known as the Tax Cuts and Jobs Act) (Pub. L. No. 115-97, 115th Cong., 1st Sess. (2017) § 11042). This limitation applies to tax years beginning after December 31, 2017, and before January 1, 2026.

[9.2] T.D. 9864 (June 11, 2019). The proposed regulations were issued as REG-112176-18 (Aug. 13, 2018). This proposal was foreshadowed by Notice 2018-54, 2018-24 I.R.B. 750.

otherwise deductible as a charitable contribution generally must be reduced by the amount of the state or local tax credit received or expected to be received.[9.3]

As an example of this body of law, a grant of a conservation easement to a county was considered to be part of a quid pro quo transaction because the transferor of the easement, a real estate developer, expected a substantial benefit in the form of an increase in value of the surrounding residential lots by reason of use of the eased property as a park.[9.4] As another illustration, the dedication of real property to a city was held to be part of a quid pro quo transaction because the purpose of the transfer was to cause the city to approve a planned community development plan, with the expectation of approval of a subsequent plan.[9.5]

p. 601, note 12. *Insert following existing text:*

The U.S. Tax Court rejected the government's assertion that donative intent was not present in a case because the donor "desired the tax benefits flowing from a charitable contribution" (Davis v. Commissioner, 109 T.C.M. 1451, 1459 (2015)); were that the law, there would be few deductible gifts.

§ 14.2 BASIC RULES

p. 602, note 15. *Delete text following sixth period.*

§ 14.4 DEDUCTIBILITY OF GIFTS TO FOUNDATIONS

p. 605, note 46. *Delete 14.3 and insert 14.1.*

p. 606, note 49. *Delete 14.5(a) and insert 14.6(a).*

p. 606, note 50. *Delete 14.4 and insert 14.5(a).*

§ 14.5 QUALIFIED APPRECIATED STOCK RULE

p. 607, last paragraph. *Insert as last sentence:*

In the most recent ruling in the first category, the IRS held that stock contributed to a private foundation by a single-member limited liability company (a disregarded entity) was qualified appreciated stock, thereby giving rise to a fair market value deduction for the two individuals who are the managers of the LLC, where one of these individuals is the sole trustee of the foundation and the settlor and trustee of a trust that is the LLC's member.[62.1]

[9.3] Prop. Reg. § 1.170A-1(h)(3)(i)-(v).

[9.4] Wendell Falls Development, LLC v. Commissioner, 115 T.C.M. 1197 (2018), supplemented by 116 T.C.M. 504 (2018).

[9.5] Triumph Mixed Use Investments LLC v. Commissioner, 115 T.C.M. 1329 (2018).

[62.1] Priv. Ltr. Rul. 201848005.

§ 14.9 ADMINISTRATIVE CONSIDERATIONS

p. 613, first complete paragraph, first sentence. *Delete and insert:*

The federal tax law contains many requirements to which donors to private foundations (or other tax-exempt charitable organizations) must adhere as a condition of receiving a charitable deduction for their contributions.

(a) Record-Keeping Rules

p. 613, note 91. *Insert before period:*

; Reg. § 1.170A-15(a)(1)

(b) Substantiation Rules

p. 613. *Insert as first paragraph of subsection, following heading:*

A charitable contribution deduction is generally not allowed for a noncash charitable contribution of less than $250 by an individual, partnership, S corporation, or C corporation that is a personal service corporation or closely held corporation, unless the donor maintains for each contribution a receipt from the donee organization showing the name and address of the donee, the date of the contributions, a description of the property, and, in the case of securities, the name of the issuer, the type of security, and whether the securities are publicly traded.[91.1]

p. 613. *In what has become fourth complete paragraph, indent first line.*

p. 613, note 92, first line. *Insert before period:*

; Reg. §§ 1.170A-15(a)(2), 1.170A-13(f)(1)

p. 613, note 93, first line. *Delete citation to regulation and insert:*

Reg. § 1.170A-13(f)(2).

p. 613, third full paragraph. *Insert as last sentence:*

A written acknowledgment is *contemporaneous* if it is obtained by the donor on or before the earlier of (1) the date the donor files the original return for the tax year in which the contribution is made or (2) the due date, including extensions, for filing the donor's original return for that year.[93.1]

p. 613, last paragraph, first line. *Insert footnote 93.2 following* **services:**

[93.2] The phrase *goods or services* means cash, property, services, benefits, and privileges (Reg. § 1.170A-13(f)(5)). Certain goods or services, however, are disregarded (Reg. § 1.170A-13(f)(8)).

[91.1] Reg. § 1.170A-16(a)(1). In certain instances, reliable written records may be substituted (Reg. § 1.170A-16(a)(2)).

[93.1] Reg. § 1.170A-13(f)(3).

p. 613, last paragraph, last line. *Delete* exchange *and insert* consideration.[93.3]

p. 614, note 94. *Delete text and insert:*

Reg. § 1.170A-13(f)(7). A *good faith estimate* means a donee organization's estimate of the fair market value of any goods or services, without regard to the manner in which the organization in fact made that estimate (*id.*).

p. 614, note 101. *Delete* No. 19 *and insert* 557.

p. 615, note 103. *Insert before period*:

; Reg. § 1.170A-16(c)(4)

p. 615, carryover paragraph. Delete last sentence, including footnote.

p. 615, first complete paragraph. *Delete and insert:*

A charitable deduction is not allowed for a noncash charitable contribution of more than $500 but not more than $5,000 by an individual, partnership, S corporation, or C corporation that is a personal services corporation or a closely held corporation unless the donor completes an IRS form and files it with the return on which the deduction is claimed.[105]

Generally, a charitable deduction is not allowed for a noncash charitable contribution of more than $5,000 unless the donor (1) substantiates the contribution with a contemporaneous written acknowledgment,[105.1] (2) obtains a qualified appraisal prepared by a qualified appraiser,[105.2] and (3) completes an IRS form[105.3] and files it with the return on which the deduction is claimed.[105.4] A qualified appraisal is not required, however, in instances of contributions of publicly traded securities, certain intellectual property, certain vehicles, and inventory and like property.[105.5] In a case, a donor lost his deduction for a charitable contribution in the amount of $338,080, reflecting a partial interest in an aircraft, by reason of these rules; he did not obtain the requisite acknowledgment from the donee and did not include the requisite information with the

---

[93.3] A donee organization provides goods or services *in consideration for* a person's payment if, at the time the person makes the payment to the donee organization, the person receives or expects to receive, goods or services in exchange for that payment (Reg. § 1.170A-13(f)(6)). Goods or services a donee organization provides in consideration for a payment by a person include goods or services provided in a year other than the year in which the person makes the payment to the organization (*id.*).

[105] IRC § 170(f)(11)(A), (B); Reg. § 1.170A-16(c)(2). The form is Form 8283 (Section A) (Reg. § 1.170A-16(c)(3)).

[105.1] See § 14.9(b).

[105.2] See § 14.9(d).

[105.3] Form 8283 (Section B).

[105.4] IRC § 170(f)(11)(C); Reg. § 1.170A-16(d)(1).

[105.5] Reg. § 1.170A-16(d)(2).

tax return involved.[105.6] In the case of noncash charitable contributions of more than $500,000, the foregoing three requirements must be met, and a copy of a qualified appraisal must be attached to the return on which the contribution is claimed.[105.7]

As noted,[105.8] if the applicable substantiation requirements are not satisfied, the charitable deduction otherwise available is not allowed.[105.9] This deduction disallowance rule does not apply, however, if it is shown to the IRS that the failure to meet the requirements is due to reasonable cause and not to willful neglect.[105.10] The U.S. Tax Court ruled that a reasonable cause inquiry is "inherently a fact-intensive one, and facts and circumstances must be judged on a case-by-case basis."[105.11] Consequently, the tax regulations do not include a standard for determining reasonable cause in this context.[105.12]

p. 615, note 111. *Delete* **14.6(b)** *and insert* **14.9(b), text accompanied by notes 92–101.**

p. 615, note 112. *Insert* **See § 16.9** *following existing text.*

(d) Appraisal Rules

p. 616, note 117. *Delete text and insert*:

Reg. § 1.170A-16(d)(1).

p. 616, note 118, first line. *Delete regulation citation and insert Id.*

p. 616, note 118, last line. *Delete* No.

p. 616, second complete paragraph, second sentence. *Delete, including footnote, and insert:*

The qualified appraisal must be signed and dated by the qualified appraiser no earlier than 60 days before the date of the contribution and no later than (1) the due date, including extensions, of the return on which the deduction for the contribution is first claimed; (2) in the case of a donor that is a partnership or S corporation, the due date, including extensions, of the return on which the deduction for the contribution is first reported; or (3) in the case of a deduction

---

[105.6] Izen, Jr. v. Commissioner, 148 T.C. 71 (2017).

[105.7] IRC § 170(f)(11)(D); Reg. § 1.170A-16(e)(1).

[105.8] See text accompanied by *supra* note 105.

[105.9] IRC § 170(f)(11)(A)(i).

[105.10] IRC § 170(f)(11)(A)(ii)(II).

[105.11] Crimi v. Commissioner, 105 T.C.M. 1330, 1353 (2013). The court concluded that the donors reasonably and in good faith relied on their long-term certified public accountant's advice that their appraisal satisfied all the legal requirements for claiming a charitable deduction.

[105.12] A standard was in these regulations in their proposed form but was omitted from the final version of the regulations because of this court decision.

first claimed on an amended return, the date on which the amended return is filed.[119]

p. 616, second complete paragraph, third sentence. *Delete, including footnote, and insert:*

A *qualified appraisal* is an appraisal document that is prepared by a qualified appraiser in accordance with generally accepted appraisal standards and meets certain other requirements.[120] The phrase *generally accepted appraisal standards* means the substance and principles of the Uniform Standards of Professional Appraisal Practice, as developed by the Appraisal Standards Board of the Appraisal Foundation.[121]

p. 616, last paragraph. *Delete, including footnotes, and insert:*

A qualified appraisal must include certain information about the contributed property, the terms of any agreement between the donor and donee as to disposition of the contributed property, the date or expected date of the contribution, certain information about the appraiser, the signature of the appraiser, the date the report was signed by the appraiser, a declaration by the appraiser, a statement that the appraisal was prepared for income tax purposes, the method of valuation used to determine fair market value, and the specific basis for the valuation.[122]

Notwithstanding the foregoing, an appraisal is not a qualified appraisal for a particular contribution if the donor failed to disclose or misrepresented facts, and a reasonable person would expect that the failure or misrepresentation would cause the appraiser to misstate the value of the contributed property.[122.1] A donor must obtain a separate qualified appraisal for each item of property for which an appraisal is required and that is not included in a group of similar items of property.[122.2] If the contributed property is a partial interest,[122.3] the

---

[119]Reg. § 1.170A-17(a)(4).

[120]IRC § 170(f)(11)(E)(i); Reg. § 1.170A-17(a)(1). A case is pending in the U.S. Tax Court as to whether a valuation report concerning shares of stock purchased by an acquiring company can constitute a qualified appraisal for use by donors who contributed shares of the issuer to a charitable organization (Chrem v. Commissioner, 116 T.C.M. 347 (2018), denying motions for summary judgment).

[121]Reg. § 1.170A-17(a)(2).

[122]Reg. § 1.170A-17(a)(3).

[122.1]Reg. § 1.170A-17(a)(6).

[122.2]Reg. § 1.170A-17(a)(7).

[122.3]See *Charitable Giving* § 9.23.

appraisal must be of the partial interest.[122.4] The fee for a qualified appraisal cannot be based to any extent on the appraised value of the property.[122.5]

p. 617, first paragraph. *Delete, including footnotes, and insert:*

A *qualified appraiser* is an individual with verifiable education and experience in valuing the type of property for which the valuation is performed. The appraiser must have (1) successfully completed professional or college-level coursework in valuing the type of property involved and have had at least two years of experience in valuing the type of property or (2) earned a recognized appraisal designation for the type of property.[123]

These individuals are not qualified appraisers for the appraised property: (1) an individual who receives a prohibited fee[124] for the appraisal of the appraised property, (2) the donor of the property, (3) a party to the transaction in which the donor acquired the property, (4) the donee of the property, (5) related parties, (6) an independent contractor who is regularly used as an appraiser by the individuals involved and who does not perform a majority of appraisals for others during the tax year, and (7) an individual who is prohibited from practicing before the IRS at any time during the three-year period ending on the date the appraisal is signed by the individual.[125]

p. 617. *Delete last paragraph.*

[122.4]Reg. § 1.170A-17(a)(12). For example, in one case, an appraiser incorrectly valued a parcel of real property rather than an easement, the subject of the gift, placed on the property (Costello v. Commissioner, 109 T.C.M. 1441 (2015)). A corollary to this rule is the rule that an appraisal must be of the gifted property. In one instance, two appraisals were held to not be qualified ones, in part because they did not appraise the correct asset; the appraisals valued the assets of a corporation where they should have valued the shares of stock of the corporation that were the subject of the gift (Estate of Evenchik v. Commissioner, 105 T.C.M. 1231 (2013)).

[122.5]Reg. § 1.170A-17(a)(9).

[123]IRC § 170(f)(11)(E)(ii); Reg. § 1.170A-17(b)(1)–(3).

[124]See text accompanied by *supra* note 120.

[125]Reg. § 1.170A-17(b)(5). An appraisal from such an appraiser will be disregarded as to value but could constitute a qualified appraisal if the requirements are otherwise satisfied and the donor did not have any knowledge that the signature, date, or declaration was false when the appraisal and Form 8283 (Section B) were signed by the appraiser (Reg. § 1.170A-17(a)(11)).

CHAPTER FIFTEEN

Private Foundations and Public Charities

§ 15.2 EVOLUTION OF LAW OF PRIVATE FOUNDATIONS

p. 626, note 28. *Insert before period:*

; Rev. Proc. 2020-5, 2020-1 I.R.B. 241 § 7.03

§ 15.3 ORGANIZATIONS WITH INHERENTLY PUBLIC ACTIVITY

(a) Churches and Similar Entities

p. 627, note 32, first line. *Delete* 1.170A-9(a) *and insert* 1.170A-9(b).

(b) Educational Institutions

p. 628, note 42, first line. *Delete* **1.170A-9(b)** *and insert* **1.170A-9(c).**

p. 629. *Insert as last paragraph:*

A court upended the foregoing requirements for qualification as an educational institution (and most of the other categories of public institutions), holding that the primary-function test and the merely-incidental test, as a matter of statutory construction, "exceed the bounds of authority" provided by the statute and thus are unlawful.[54.1] The court based this finding on its conclusion that Congress "unambiguously chose not to include a primary-function requirement" in the statutory definition of *educational organization*.[54.2] That conclusion was, in turn, based on the fact that the "equivalent of that very requirement"[54.3] appears in the federal tax law concerning public charity hospitals.[54.4] The heart of this part of the analysis is the rule of statutory construction that, in determining whether statutory language is plain and unambiguous, a court must read all parts of the statute together and give full effect to each part.[54.5] The court might have arrived at a different decision if it had applied another construction rule, which is that the judicial interpreter is to consider the entire text, in view of its structure and of the physical and logical relation of its many parts.[54.6] The problem is that this decision interprets the law of public charities in a way that enables an entity to qualify as a public charity simply by tangentially qualifying.[54.7]

[54.1] Mayo Clinic v. United States, 412 F. Supp. 3d 1038, 1057 (D. Minn. 2019) (on appeal).

[54.2] *Id*. at 1047.

[54.3] *Id*.

[54.4] See § 15.3(c).

[54.5] This is one of the *contextual canons* used in construing statutes; it is a *presumption of consistent usage*. See Scalia and Garner, *Reading Law: The Interpretation of Legal Texts* 170 (Thomson/West, St. Paul, MN, 2012).

[54.6] This is the *whole-text canon* (*Reading Law, supra* note 54.5, at 1167). In this case, the court did not read "all parts of the statute together"; it read only two sections of it (IRC § 170(b)(1)(A)(ii) and (iii)). The entire statute is IRC § 170(b)(1)(A), where the law provides for nine categories of public charities, eight of which do not contain the primary-function requirement. It is probable that the writers of the statute had a reason to insert the requirement only in IRC § 170(b)(1)(A)(iii), a point the court did not explore.

[54.7] The IRS calculated that the Mayo Clinic's educational activities were only 13 percent of its total activities and that its revenue from educational undertakings was merely 6 percent of total revenue (Tech. Adv. Mem. 201407024). The court in this case may have violated another contextual canon: the *absurdity doctrine*. This canon states that a provision may be judicially corrected where the failure to do so would result in a disposition that no reasonable person could approve (*Reading Law, supra* note 54.5, at 234.) Indeed, another contextual canon the court should have applied is the *harmonious-reading canon*, pursuant to which the provisions of a text should be interpreted in a way that renders them compatible, not contradictory (*id*., at 180).

(c) Hospitals

p. 630, note 60. *Delete* 1.170A-9(c)(1) *and insert* 1.170A-9(d)(1).

p. 630, note 63. *Delete* 1.170A-9(c)(1) *and insert* 1.170A-9(d)(1).

(d) Medical Research Organizations

p. 631, note 64. *Delete* 1.170A-9(c)(2)(iii) *and insert* 1.170A-9(d)(2)(iii).

p. 631, note 65. *Delete* 1.170A-9(c)(2)(iv) *and insert* 1.170A-9(d)(2)(iv).

p. 631, note 66. *Delete* 1.170A-9(c)(2)(vii) *and insert* 1.170A-9(d)(2)(vii).

p. 631, note 67. *Delete* 1.170A-9(c)(2)(vi)(a) *and insert* 1.170A-9(d)(2)(vi)(a).

p. 631, note 68. *Delete* 1.170A-9(c)(2)(v)(b) *and insert* 1.170A-9(d)(2)(v)(b).

p. 631, note 69, first line. *Delete* 1.170A-9(c)(2)(v)(c) *and insert* 1.170A-9(d)(2)(v)(c).

(f) Public College Support Foundations

p. 632, note 74. *Delete* 1.170A-9(b)(2) *and insert* 1.170A-9(c)(2).

(g) Governmental Units

p. 633, note 77. *Delete* 1.170A-9(d) *and insert* 1.170A-9(e).

§ 15.4 PUBLICLY SUPPORTED ORGANIZATIONS—DONATIVE ENTITIES

(a) General Rules

p. 634, note 86, first line. *Delete* 1.170A-9(e)(1)(ii) *and insert* 1.170A-9(f)(1)(ii).

p. 636, note 92. *Delete* 1.170A-9(e)(6)(i) *and insert* 1.170A-9(f)(6)(i).

p. 636, note 98, first line. *Delete* 1.170A-9(e)(6)(v) *and insert* 1.170A-9(f)(6)(v).

(b) Support Test

p. 638, note 109. *Delete* 1.170A-9(e)(7)(i) *and insert* 1.170A-9(f)(7)(i).

p. 638, note 113. *Delete* 1.170A-9(e)(6) *and insert* 1.170A-9(f)(6).

p. 638, note 114. *Delete* 1.170A-9(e)(7)(i) *and insert* 1.170A-9(f)(7)(i).

p. 638, note 115. *Delete* 1.170A-9(e)(7)(ii) *and insert* 1.170A-9(f)(7)(ii).

p. 638, note 116. *Delete* 1.170A-9(e)(6)(ii), (iii) *and insert* 1.170A-9(f)(6)(ii), (iii).

p. 639, note 117. *Delete* 1.170A-9(e)(4)(i) *and insert* 1.170A-9(f)(4)(i).

p. 639, note 120, first line. *Delete* 170A-9(e)(7)(iii) *and insert* 1.170A-9(f)(7)(iii).

p. 639, note 121, first line. *Delete* 1.170A-9(e)(8) *and insert* 1.170A-9(f)(8).

p. 640, note 122, first line. *Delete* 1.170A-9(e)(7)(ii) *and insert* 1.170A-9(f)(7)(ii).

p. 641. *Insert following first complete paragraph, before heading:*

A tax-exempt charitable organization with more than one unrelated business may aggregate its net income and net losses from all unrelated businesses for purposes of determining whether the organization is publicly supported under these rules.[126.1] That is, the bucketing rule[126.2] does not apply in this context.

(c) Facts and Circumstances Test

p. 642, note 127, first line. *Delete* 1.170A-9(e)(3) *and insert* 1.170A-9(f)(3).

(d) Community Foundations

p. 643, note 129. *Delete* 1.170A-9(e)(4)(v), 1.170A-9(e)(6)(iv) *and insert* 1.170A-9(f)(4)(v), 1.170A-9(f)(6)(iv).

p. 643, note 130. *Delete* 1.170A-9(e)(10) *and insert* 1.170A-9(f)(10).

p. 643, note 133. *Delete* 1.170A-9(e)(10) *and insert* 1.170A-9(f)(10).

p. 644, note 135. *Delete* 1.170A-9(e)(11)(ii) *and insert* 1.170A-9(f)(11)(ii).

p. 644, note 136, first line. *Delete* 1.170A-9(e)(11)(iii)-(vi) *and insert* 1.170A-9(f)(11)(iii)-(vi).

p. 644, note 137, first line. *Delete* 1.170A-9(e)(11)(v) *and* 1.170A-9(e)(14) *and insert* 1.170A-9(f)(11)(v) *and* 1.170A-9(f)(14).

§ 15.5 SERVICE PROVIDER ORGANIZATIONS

(a) Investment Income Test

p. 647. *Insert as third complete paragraph:*

A tax-exempt charitable organization with more than one unrelated business may aggregate its net income and net losses from all unrelated businesses for purposes of determining whether the organization is publicly supported

---

[126.1]Prop. Reg. § 1.170A-9(f)(7)(v).
[126.2]See § 11.5(b).

■ 104 ■

under these rules.[166.1] That is, the bucketing rule[166.2] does not apply in this context.

(c) Unusual Grants

p. 651, first complete paragraph. *Insert as last sentence:*

In still another instance, a proposed grant was ruled to constitute an unusual grant; it indeed had an unusual feature, which was that the grant request was made by an unrelated third party, without the private foundation's knowledge.[187.1]

p. 652. *Insert as third and fourth paragraphs:*

A private foundation proposed a grant to a public charity to provide permanent support for two of the charity's core programs. There would not be any material restrictions or conditions regarding this grant other than typical restrictions concerning establishment and maintenance of an endowment fund. The foundation previously granted a substantial part of the charity's financial support. The IRS concluded that, due to the historic relationship between the parties, the proposed grant is not "unusual or unexpected."[191.1] Indeed, the IRS added, "[s]ubsequent grants from the same donor [i.e., grantor] are logically more usual and more expected."

A tax-exempt charitable organization provided injured special operations combat veterans with outdoor recreational programs to, in part, encourage and foster rehabilitation, recovery, and transition. Having learned of these programs, an organization allowed this entity use of its property in furtherance of these veterans' assistance programs. Now this entity is dissolving and wants to distribute its remaining assets to this veterans' organization. Ruling that this assets transfer would be an unusual grant, the IRS held that the prior relationship between the entities, concerning use of the land, was "incidental" and, although there was some board overlap, the veterans' group had sufficient independent members. In so ruling, the IRS said that the transfer was in the nature of a bequest.[191.2]

p. 653, second complete paragraph. *Delete and insert:*

[166.1] Prop. Reg. § 1.509(a)-3(a)(3)(i), (4).
[166.2] See § 11.5(b).
[187.1] Priv. Ltr. Rul. 201952009.
[191.1] Priv. Ltr. Rul. 201850023.
[191.2] Priv. Ltr. Rul. 201923027.

A request for advance approval that a prospective grant or contribution constitutes an unusual grant must be submitted to the IRS by filing an IRS form.[196.1]

p. 653, third complete paragraph. *Insert as last sentence:*

Likewise, a supporting organization was merging into a supported organization,[198.1] transferring cash, marketable securities, venture capital, and private equity investments; the IRS ruled that this distribution will be an unusual grant, in part because the "size and method of [the] contribution is unusual compared to [the organization's] typical level of support" and the transfer was a "one-time occurrence."[198.2]

§ 15.7 SUPPORTING ORGANIZATIONS

(g) Operated in Connection with (Type III)

p. 670, third paragraph, first sentence. *Delete and insert:*

The federal tax law provides for two categories of Type III supporting organizations.

p. 675, note 350. *Insert following existing text:*

A supporting organization, in the aftermath of publication of the final regulations embodying these rules, determined that "it could be run more efficiently as a private foundation"; it settled its relationship with its supported organizations and successfully converted to foundation status (Priv. Ltr. Rul. 201825004).

§ 15.8 CHANGE OF PUBLIC CHARITY CATEGORY

(a) From § 509(a)(1) to § 509(a)(2) or Vice Versa

p. 688, first complete paragraph. *Delete and insert:*

The sources of financial support of a publicly supported charity may change, causing it to fail to qualify under the category of publicly supported charity recognized in its determination letter, yet begin to qualify under another category of publicly supported charity. For example, an organization may commence operations qualifying as a donative publicly supported charity,[413.1] then subsequently become qualified only as a service provider publicly supported charity.[413.2] In this circumstance, the charitable organization must

---

[196.1]Form 8940, along with a $500 user fee (Rev. Proc. 2020-5, 2020-1 I.R.B. 241 § 4.02(6)(e)).
[198.1]See § 15.7.
[198.2]Priv. Ltr. Rul. 201909015.
[413.1]See § 15.4.
[413.2]See § 15.5.

decide whether to report the change in public charity status on its annual information return or seek recognition of the new public charity status.[413.3]

(b)   From § 509(a)(3) to § 509(a)(1) or § 509(a)(2)

p. 688, second complete paragraph, first sentence. *Delete and insert:*

A charitable organization classified as a supporting organization[413.4] may receive revenues that enable it to qualify as a donative publicly supported charity or a service provider publicly supported charity.

p. 688, note 415. *Delete text and insert:*

See § 15.8(d).

(d)   IRS Recognition of Change in Status

p. 689, first complete paragraph, first line. *Delete* issued *and insert* annually issues.

p. 689, note 418. *Delete text and insert:*

Currently, Rev. Proc. 2020-5, 2020-1 I.R.B. 241.

p. 689, second complete paragraph, third line. *Delete* IRS *and insert* [IRS].

p. 689, second complete paragraph, fifth line. *Insert footnote* **481.1** *following period:*

[418.1] Rev. Proc. 2020-5, 2020-1 I.R.B. 241 § 7.04(1).

p. 689, second complete paragraph, last sentence. *Delete and insert:*

A public charity seeks recognition of a change in public charity status, or of a change from public charity status to private foundation status,[418.2] by filing an IRS form.[418.3]

p. 689, third complete paragraph, second line. *Delete last* IRS *and insert* its.

p. 689, third complete paragraph, third line. *Insert* determination *following* new.

p. 689, third complete paragraph, third line. *Insert footnote* **418.4** *following period:*

[418.4] Rev. Proc. 2020-5, 2020-1 I.R.B. 241 § 7.04(4).

[413.3] See § 15.8(d).

[413.4] See § 15.7.

[418.2] *Id.* § 7.04(2).

[418.3] Form 8940, along with a user fee of $500 (Rev. Proc. 2020-5, 2020-1 I.R.B. 241 §§ 4.02(6)(g), 7.04).

p. 689, note 421, second and third lines. *Delete* 2018-5, 2018-1 I.R.B. 235 *and insert* 2019-5, 2019-1 I.R.B. 230.

p. 689. *Insert as fifth complete paragraph, before heading:*

A charitable organization that erroneously determined that it was a private foundation[421.1] and wishes to correct the error can request a determination letter classifying it as a public charity by showing that it continuously met the public support tests during the relevant period.[421.2]

§ 15.9 NONCHARITABLE SUPPORTED ORGANIZATIONS

p. 690, second paragraph, eleventh line. *Insert footnote* 423.1 *following* **tax-exempt:**

[423.1] E.g., Priv. Ltr. Rul. 201844013.

p. 690, second paragraph, last line. *Insert footnote at end of line:*

[423.2] An illustration of the need to use a supporting organization, to house substantial charitable and educational activities, in connection with an exempt business league, appears in Priv. Ltr. Rul. 202017035.

[421.1] For example, an organization may erroneously classify an item or items in its calculation of public support.

[421.2] Rev. Proc. 2019-5, 2019-1 I.R.B. 230 § 7.04(3).

CHAPTER SIXTEEN

Donor-Advised Funds

§ 16.1 BASIC DEFINITIONS

p. 699, note 4. *Insert following existing text:*

For additional and updated statistics, see § 16.13.

§ 16.3 TYPES OF DONOR FUNDS

p. 701, note 19. *Delete* 22 *and insert* 27.

§ 16.9 STATUTORY CRITERIA

p. 717, note 119. *Insert following existing text:*

A lawsuit has been filed against an organization sponsoring donor-advised funds, alleging that the organization sold stock contributed for a fund despite having promised it would hold the stock and sell it gradually as the securities appreciated in value (Fairbairn v. Fidelity Investments Charitable Gift Fund, Case No. 3:18-cv-4881 (Aug. 10, 2018)). The sponsoring organization's position is that it is the organization's policy to sell securities immediately on receipt and that the plaintiffs were aware of the policy. A commentary on this litigation states that the case is a "challenge to how the funds are becoming the dominant charitable behemoths in the United States" and "has the potential to cool a fast-growing area of charitable giving" (Sullivan, "Lawsuit Could Cool a Fast-Growing Way of Giving to Charities," *New York Times*, May 31, 2019).

§ 16.12 TAX REGULATIONS

(f) Fidelity Gift Fund Comments

p. 727, last line. *Insert footnote 123 at end of line:*

[123] An organization recognized as an exempt religious and charitable entity administered several programs, at least some of which were in furtherance of a "church planting movement." It provides a "valuable opportunity for people involved in ministry who would like to be involved in doing independent ministry or working for an approved charitable project." The agent's report stated that this organization acted as a sponsoring organization for a number of donor-advised funds. Elsewhere in the report, however, it was said that these funds do not qualify as donor-advised funds. The report stated that donor-advised funds "have specific rules and regulations that must be met"; it added "[t]hese regulations are precise and specific." (The report did not reference or discuss these rules; there are no "regulations" in this context.) The organization had its exemption revoked basically because it was "unable to provide sufficient documentation to show that at the time of disbursements it had sufficient discretion and control over funds expended" (Priv. Ltr. Rul. 201922038).

p. 727. *Insert following existing text:*

§ 16.13 DAF STATISTICAL PORTRAIT

According to the National Philanthropic Trust, for the eighth consecutive year, "there was growth in all key metrics" concerning donor-advised funds: "number of individual donor-advised funds, total grant dollars from them, total contributions to them and total charitable assets in them."[124]

Charitable giving in the United States in 2017 is estimated to have totaled $410.02 billion; giving by individuals in that year amounted to an estimated $286.65 billion, constituting 70 percent of all charitable giving for the year.[125] Contributions to donor-advised funds totaled $29.23 billion in 2017, representing 10.2 percent of individual giving in that year.

In 2017, there were 463,622 donor-advised funds, with assets totaling $110.01 billion. The average size of donor-advised funds was $237,356. Grants from donor-advised funds totaled $19.08 billion,[126] with a payout rate of 22.1 percent. By contrast, in 2017, there were 82,516 private foundations, with assets valued at $855.81 billion. Grants from private foundations totaled 49.5 billion in that year.

The National Philanthropic Trust classifies sponsoring organizations as being in one of three categories: national charities, community foundations, and single-issue charities.

---

[124] National Philanthropic Trust, "The 2018 Donor-Advised Fund Report" (permission granted as to use of content).

[125] Tax-Exempt Organizations, § 2.1.

[126] This level of grantmaking, a new high, is a 19.9 percent increase from the 2016 level of $15.91 billion.

National charities[127] numbered 53. They had a total of 338,141 donor-advised funds in 2017, with combined assets of $58.58 billion. The value of grants from these funds totaled $10.3 billion. Contributions to them totaled $18.54 billion. The payout rate for these funds was 22.9 percent. The average fund size for this category was $173,241.

There are 604 community foundations.[128] They had 70,215 donor-advised funds in 2017, with combined assets of $38.61 billion. The value of grants from these funds totaled $5.78 billion. Contributions to them totaled $6.76 billion. The payout rate for these funds was 19.2 percent. The average fund size for this category was $549,840.

Single-issue charities[129] numbered 345. They had 55,266 donor-advised funds in 2017, with combined assets of $12.82 billion. The value of grants from these funds totaled $3.01 billion. Contributions to them totaled $3.93 billion. The payout rate for these funds was 26.2 percent. The average fund size for this category was $231,990.

The National Philanthropic Trust observed that "[a]ggregate payout rates have been near or above 20 percent since [it] first started collecting data in 2007," "suggest[ing] that donors who use this type of charitable giving vehicle are supporting philanthropic organizations and the public good with a consistent level of grantmaking." The Trust predicted a "continued increase in grantmaking and a possible increase in payout rates."

The largest of the national charities with a donor-advised fund program is the Fidelity Investments Charitable Gift Fund. It is also the first and oldest of these national charities, commencing operations in 1991. It has helped donors support more than 278,000 charitable entities with nearly $35 billion in grants.[130]

In 2018, characterized by Fidelity Charitable as a year of "uncertainty related to tax reform and volatility in the markets," the charity granted more than $5.2 billion to charity, fueled by funding by 204,292 donors. This grant-making consisted of nearly 1.3 million donor-advised grants, made to 142,515 grantees. The average fund account entailed more than 10 recommendations annually, almost twice the average 10 years ago.

During that year, more than 50 percent of the contributions to Fidelity Charitable were in the form of securities that appreciated in value. Contributions

---

[127]National charities are tax-exempt charitable organizations with a national focus in fundraising and grantmaking. They include independent organizations (such as the Trust) and charitable entities affiliated with financial institutions.

[128]See § 15.4(d).

[129]Single-issue charities are tax-exempt charitable organizations that work in a specific topic area, such as colleges and universities, faith-based charities, and issue-specific charities.

[130]Fidelity Charitable 2019 Giving Report.

of nonpublicly traded assets in the year had more than $1 billion in value; these assets included private stock, limited partnership interests, real estate, and cryptocurrency.[131]

As of that year, this sponsoring organization maintained 123,114 donor-advised funds, with a $17,670 median account balance. Seventy-two percent of the grants were made to charities the donors previously supported. Almost one-third of the grants were for educational purposes, followed by society benefit (18 percent), religion (15 percent), human services (11 percent), health (8 percent), arts and culture (7 percent), environment and animals (5 percent), and international affairs (5 percent).

In 2018, Fidelity Charitable made more than 4,000 donor-recommended grants to impact-investing charitable organizations, totaling $22.1 million. During that year, there was a 16-percent increase in charitable dollars allocated to impact investments and a 10-percent increase in the number of grants to impact-investment charitable entities.

§ 16.14 CRITICISMS AND COMMENTARY

Donor-advised funds are one of nonprofit law's hottest topics. Although they have been in existence for decades and controversial for years, the level of controversy is intensifying as the amount of giving to donor-advised funds continues to rise rapidly, private foundations make greater use of these funds, and the federal government's regulatory apparatus begins to seriously focus on them. This increase in controversy is sparking growth in the ranks of donor-advised funds' advocates and critics, which stokes still more controversy.

Every statistic demonstrates the dramatic increase in utilization of donor-advised funds: the sheer number of them, the size of the larger sponsoring organizations, the amount of giving to donor-advised funds, and the amounts of grants from these funds.[132] There are record-breaking analyses of donor-advised funds, many articles about them, and more presentations about them at nonprofit law conferences.

The government's tax law establishment has, for decades, been suspicious of donor-advised funds, believing them to be vehicles to sidestep the private foundation rules. This is seen as nefarious, if not outright illegal, behavior. In fact, donor-advised funds are an alternative to private foundations—in most legitimate and effective ways.

---

[131] This development is reflective of the fact of emergence of a new service provided by sponsoring organizations: conversion of "complex assets" into money for purposes of grantmaking.

[132] See § 16.13.

Foes of donor-advised funds have never been able to get beyond the notion that these funds are fundamentally flawed and thus tarnished because they are rested on a *legal fiction*. The "fiction" is that sponsoring organizations own and control the contributed money. The "reality," from the critics' viewpoint, is that the true control remains with the donors, inasmuch as the "advice" proffered by them is not really "advice" at all since it is nearly always followed by the sponsors. All of this is seen, in these quarters, as nothing more than wealthy individuals playing economic games at the expense of charities serving the poor and downtrodden. Often, the concept of this legal fiction devolves into portrayals using words such as *loophole* and *sham*.

Opponents of donor-advised funds are also unhappy because there can be a delay between the making of a charitable contribution and use of the money for charitable ends. This is indisputably true. The same can be said, however, with respect to gifts to other charitable vehicles, such as private foundations, supporting organizations, and charitable remainder trusts. (Of course, these entities also have their critics.)

By 2018, when levels of contributions to donor-advised funds began reaching spectacular heights, critics of donor-advised funds had worked themselves into an anti-donor-advised fund frenzy, the likes of which the nonprofit world had never seen before.[133] Advocates of donor-advised funds, by contrast, were rather quiet. Critics of these funds were blasting them in all forms of media, using inflammatory terminology in an effort to force further federal regulation of donor-advised funds. Here is a sampling:

- *The Chronicle of Philanthropy*, in November, 2014, published an article titled "A Gain to Commercial Funds Is a Loss to Charities."

- *Atlantic*, in May, 2018, ran an article titled "The 'Black Hole' That Sucks Up Silicon Valley's Money."

- *Forbes*, in May, 2018, published an article titled "Foundations of Hedge Fund Managers Gave Big to Controversial Donor-Advised Funds."

- The Institute for Policy Studies, in July, 2018, published a report titled "Warehousing Wealth: Donor-Advised Charity Funds Sequestering Billions in the Face of Growing Inequality."

- The *Nonprofit Quarterly*, in its Summer 2018 issue, published three articles critical of donor-advised funds, one of which is titled "Three

---

[133]Private foundations certainly endured serious and ongoing criticism in the years leading up to enactment of the Tax Reform Act of 1969 (see §§ 1.1, 1.3), but the vitriol level is higher in the case of donor-advised funds.

Simple Steps to Protect Charities and American Taxpayers from the Rise of Donor-Advised Funds."

- The *New York Times*, in August, 2018, ran an article with the headline "How Tech Billionaires Hack Their Taxes With a Philanthropic Loophole."

- Paul Streckfus, in his *EO Tax Journal*, in August, 2018, wrote that "[a]ll of us need to keep beating the drums and demanding legislative action because the alternative is moral bankruptcy for the entire nonprofit sector."

- In August, 2018, a law professor blogged that "you first must begin with the self-evidently true factual proposition that the independence of the DAF from the donor is a sham."

- The *Chronicle of Philanthropy* published an article in August, 2018, with the title "How I Helped Create the Donor-Advised Fund Monster—Inadvertently."

- Bloomberg BNA, in October, 2018, published an article titled "The Super-Rich Are Stockpiling Wealth in Black-Box Charities."

Criticisms of donor-advised funds may be collected by this composite (which has its overlaps): Donor-advised funds (1) are nefarious and illegitimate, to the point that they are shams; (2) are based on a legal fiction; (3) are loopholes; (4) involve transfers that are not really gifts; (5) are vehicles involving merely the warehousing (or stockpiling) of money; (6) are not authentic charitable programs; (7) are diverting monies from truly charitable ends; (8) are a sidestepping of the private foundation rules; (9) by using the services of related investment companies, are violating the private inurement or private benefit doctrines; (10) that are "commercial" or "national" in nature are inherently evil; (11) amount to a hijacking of philanthropy by Wall Street; (12) lack transparency; (13) do not pay out sufficient funds to real (or working) charities; and (14) are immoral, unethical, and contrary to public policy.

Inasmuch as the concept of the donor-advised fund is now codified,[134] with the statutory definition not that much different from the common-law one,[135] the contention that donor-advised funds are shams, loopholes, or legal fictions

---

[134]See § 16.9.

[135]E.g., National Foundation, Inc. v. United States, 87-2 U.S.T.C. ¶ 9602 (Ct. Cl. 1987) (see § 16.4); Priv. Ltr. Ruls. 200149045 (referencing a "charitable gift fund" with "donor-advised account[s]") (Aug. 3, 2001) and 9807030 (Nov. 19, 1997).

is not, as a matter of law, credible.[136] This fact is underscored by the gift substantiation requirement.[137]

As to the notion that transfers to sponsoring organizations, to be deposited in donor-advised funds, are not authentic gifts, that battle has been fought and its advocates vanquished.[138] Again, every donor to a sponsoring organization, if a charitable deduction is desired, must by statute be provided a notice by the organization that it has "exclusive legal control" over the funds or assets contributed,[139] a hallmark characteristic of a gift.

Then there is the contention that donor-advised funds are "warehousing" or "stockpiling" charitable dollars.[140] It is not clear why this concept of an intermediary between a donor and the ultimate donee is any different from the comparable use of private foundations, supporting organizations, charitable remainder trusts, and endowment funds. Many donors are "institutionalizing" their charitable giving these days, rather than simply making gifts without any further involvement; that appears to be a positive trend. It appears that this approach is attracting charitable gifts that would not otherwise be made, with donor-advised funds the driver of this type of philanthropic funding.[141]

---

[136]For example, one commentator raised the question as to whether donor-advised funds are "substitutes for private foundations" and thus a "loophole that avoids the private foundation anti-abuse rules?" (Colinvaux, "Donor Advised Funds: Charitable Spending Vehicles for 21st Century Philanthropy," 92 *Wash. L. Rev.* 39, 41 (2017)); another observed that donor-advised funds "are too often seen by tax planners as a work-around for the anti-abuse rules of private foundations" (Zerbe, "DAF Reform—A Chance to Provide Real Benefit to Working Charities," 25 *Nonprofit Quar.* (No. 2) 52, 55 (Summer 2018)).

[137]See § 16.9, text accompanied by note 116.

[138]See §§ 16.2, 16.4. Yet, critics still invoke the argument. E.g., the "role of the donor in this arrangement has always been treated with a wink and a nod" (Cantor, "A Gain to Commercial Funds Is a Loss to Charities," 27 *Chronicle of Philanthropy* (No. 2) 29 (Nov. 6, 2019)); private foundations make grants to donor-advised funds to satisfy the mandatory payout rules "while still retaining ongoing control over the distributed property" (Madoff, "Three Simple Steps to Protect Charities and American Taxpayers from the Rise of Donor-Advised Funds," 25 *Nonprofit Quar.* (No. 2) 46, 47 (Summer 2018)).

[139]See § 16.9, text accompanied by note 116.

[140]E.g., Woolley, "The Super-Rich Are Stockpiling Wealth in Black-Box Charities," Bloomberg BNA (Oct. 3, 2018); Institute for Policy Studies, "Warehousing Wealth: Donor-Advised Charity Funds Sequestering Billions in the Face of Growing Inequality" (July 2018). By contrast, one commentator referred to donor-advised funds as "charitable spending vehicles" (see *supra* note 136). The community foundation sector stated that it does "not concur in the view that DATs are used for 'asset parking' and are thus inherently suspect," adding that "[w]hile it may be mathematically possible for a small percentage of DAFs with very high payouts to skew an overall payout rate, that's not how things work at community foundations" (Community Foundation Public Awareness Initiative submission to House Committee on Ways and Means (July 14, 2014) (CFPAI 2014 Submission)).

[141]Gifts to donor-advised funds constituted 10 percent of individual giving in 2017 (see § 16.13). An analysis of the donor-advised fund landscape from the community foundation subsector stated that these foundations want to convert donors "from *charitable givers* to *philanthropists*"

Related to this contention is the criticism that donor-advised funds are not really engaged in charitable undertakings, such as the argument that they are to be differentiated from "working charities."[142]

Critics' favorite proposal in this connection is the mandatory payout.[143] Some see a payout requirement for donor-advised funds on an account-by-account basis as the "easy solution."[144] Others would confine a payout rule to the "national" sponsoring organizations, contending that, as one commentator observed, "[i]t should be within the competence of these sophisticated financial intermediaries to track subaccount balances and payouts over time, without creating an undue burden."[145]

If there were to be a mandatory payout, applicable to each donor-advised fund, what would it be? Some advocate using the private foundation 5 percent mechanism.[146] Then the question becomes, why have such a payout obligation in this context? The data shows that the payout rate for "national charities" is 22.9 percent, for community foundations is 19.2 percent, and for "single-issue" charities is 26.2 percent.[147] Also, it is one thing to impose a payout on organizations; it is another matter to mandate a payout for nearly 500,000 accounts.[148]

One analysis of a mandatory payout in this context raised seven points. One, if the objective of a payout requirement is to increase the amount of money dispensed from donor-advised funds, a payout rule would "have exactly the opposite impact over the medium to long term." Two, the effect of this type of proposal would be communication to the public that the concept of an endowment is reserved "only for large institutions and the very wealthy." Three, such a proposal "implies that inactive donor-advised funds are a significant public policy problem that requires attention, but the vast majority of DAF advisors are making grants regularly." Four, the proposal would establish a "structure where donor-advised funds are treated more harshly than other forms of endowments, which will be complicated and confusing to donors, as well as create an administrative nightmare for community foundations and other DAF administrators." Five, a forced payout (or spend-down) would require sponsoring organizations to "go to court to undo thousands of legal arrangements and potentially put some community foundations in violation of state law and the donor's intent." Six, the proposal "seems to imply that DAFs only provide

---

(Kridler, Philipp, Slutsky, Seleznow, and Williams, "Donor-Advised Funds: How to Make Sure They Strengthen Our Communities," *Nonprofit Quar.* (Aug. 20, 2018) (Kridler et al. Analysis)).

[142]See *supra* note 136.

[143]"Payout is the cornerstone of DAF reforms" (Zerbe, *supra* note 136, at 53).

[144]*Id.*

[145]Colinvaux, *supra* note 136, at 70.

[146]See § 6.4.

[147]See § 16.13.

[148]*Id.*

value to the community when money is 'paid out,' but at least where most community foundations are concerned, that is not the case." Seven, a payout on donor-advised funds would "make it nearly impossible for DAF advisors to engage in the rapidly growing field of 'impact investing'[149] via their DAFs."[150]

One of the few objective reviews of this matter of additional regulation of donor-advised funds concluded that it "is by no means convinced that there is widespread abuse in donor-advised funds," but adds that "conditions" exist for "widespread abuse."[151] This analysis stated: "There are two categories of concern that some advocates would like to see answered with regulation: the first has to do with the establishment of systems of accountability that look into the transactions of individual funds, and the second is what such a sight line might reveal—for example, overvaluation of noncash contributions, inactivity in disbursement of funds, and transfers of funds from private foundations in an attempt to bypass their payout rates."[152]

Another review of this subject attempted to separate myths from fact. To those who assert that donor-advised funds merely accumulate charitable gifts and are a barrier to direct support of operating charities, this analysis pointed out that "[a] number of sponsoring organizations themselves are operating public charities, offering significant social service and educational programs." In response to the charge that sponsoring organizations do not interact with donors or adequately supervise grants, the review's response was that "philanthropic professionals engage in ongoing conversations with DAF funders to learn about the donors' philanthropic passions and to provide information about grant opportunities and emerging charitable programs" and "adhere to guidelines regarding permissible grants which ensure that such distributions further" charitable objectives. To those who assert that donor-advised funds stymie philanthropic innovations, this review stated that "[m]any DAFs have existed for decades and have been characterized by regular donations as well as charitable grants from such accounts." Regarding the notion that donor-advised funds are "cloaked in anonymity," the review observed that "[s]ome donors prefer grants from DAFs to remain anonymous, but such grants are rare and are based on personal values and legitimate concerns." As to the myth that donor-advised funds divert monies from operating charities, the

---

[149]See § 8.2(g).

[150]CFPAI 2014 Submission.

[151]McCambridge, "Do Donor-Advised Funds Require Regulatory Attention?," 25 *Nonprofit Quar.* (No. 2) 41 (Summer 2018).

[152]*Id.* Overvaluations of gifted property is a subject that cuts across every mode of charitable giving; it certainly is not confined to gifts to donor-advised funds. Private foundations make grants to donor-advised funds for many reasons other than an effort to "bypass" their payout obligation (see § 16.12(c)).

response was that "[f]or many mission-based public charities, DAFs provide a ready reserve to sustain charitable activities during times of need."[153]

Community foundations—the entities that launched the donor-advised fund movement[154]—are understandably concerned about proposed "reforms" in this area, inasmuch as these funds are "vehicle[s] that raise[] billions in charitable donations to provide critical services and solve important problems in communities across the country."[155] From the standpoint of community foundations, donor-advised funds "are not standalone entities, but one important arrow in the quiver to accomplish [their] work."[156] These foundations are "concerned that some of the most vocal critics of DAFs have not worked directly with donors to understand their motivations and behaviors."[157] They issued this plea: "[I]t's important to make sure we are thoughtful and deliberate and that any changes will not bring unintended consequences in the form of decreased charitable giving."[158] Other potential unwanted consequences in this regard are "government overreach, excessive regulation, and bureaucratic waste."[159]

Critics of donor-advised funds have, so far, dominated the debate over donor-advised funds. This phenomenon has had unfortunate consequences. One of these consequences is an overlooking of the fact that donor-advised funds are one of many charitable giving vehicles, sharing several of the same characteristics (as intermediaries), principally private foundations, supporting organizations, charitable remainder trusts, and endowment funds.[160] Another of these consequences is a general failure of public charities to adequately integrate donor-advised funds into their fundraising program. One of the few analyses of this point observed that the existence of these funds enhances the "charitable conversation between advisers and [donor] clients," helps "donors make wise giving decisions," and facilitates "even bigger contributions than the nonprofit [organizations] would have otherwise received."[161] This analysis

---

[153]Beckwith and Woolf, "Donor-Advised Funds: Separating Myth from Fact," reproduced in the *EO Tax Journal* (Oct. 19, 2018).

[154]See the introduction to this chapter.

[155]Kridler et al. Analysis.

[156]*Id.*

[157]*Id.*

[158]*Id.*

[159]*Id.* A look at the statutory law and accompanying regulations concerning Type III supporting organizations (see § 15.7(g)) results in confirmation of the validity of these fears.

[160]See the text accompanied by *supra* note 156. These vehicles are compared and contrasted in Hopkins, *How To Be a Successful Philanthropist: Avoiding the Legal Pitfalls* (Pittsburgh, PA: Dorrance Publishing, 2018).

[161]Nopar, "Savvy Nonprofits Can Reap Big Benefits," 27 *Chronicle of Philanthropy* (No. 2) 29, 32 (Nov. 6, 2014).

concluded: "Everybody in the nonprofit world should support any technique that creates more opportunities for charitable giving."[162]

An analysis of donor-advised funds posits the amply reasonable assumption that "interest in these giving vehicles will continue, as will debates about how they should be regulated."[163] This report concluded: "Donor-advised funds are here to stay for the foreseeable future."[164]

---

[162]*Id.*

[163]Giving USA, "The Data on Donor-Advised Funds: New Insights You Need to Know" (2018), at 36.

[164]*Id.*

CHAPTER SEVENTEEN

Corporate Foundations

p. 732. *Insert following first complete paragraph, before heading:*

§ 17.3A   PRIVATE BENEFIT DOCTRINE

Private foundations are also subject to the doctrine of private benefit.[19.1] This doctrine is infrequently applied in the corporate foundation context, however, because the self-dealing rules or the private benefit doctrine usually take precedence.

    A rare instance involving the private benefit doctrine in this context concerned the Panera Bread Foundation, which operated the Panera Cares Cafes. The Foundation's view is that this program provided food to the needy and provided job training to high-risk individuals and those with developmental disabilities. The IRS proposed to retroactively revoke the tax-exempt status of the Foundation, on the grounds of unwarranted private benefit and violation of the commerciality doctrine.[19.2] Thereafter, the Foundation filed a petition in the U.S. Tax Court seeking continuation of its exemption, noting that the cafes operating in only five of Panera's 2,000-plus stores had been closed.[19.3] Subsequently, the Tax Court issued a stipulated opinion enabling the Foundation to retain its exempt status.[19.4]

[19.1] See § 5.2.
[19.2] Priv. Ltr. Rul. 201911010.
[19.3] Panera Bread Foundation, Inc. v. Commissioner, Docket No. 5198-19X (filed Mar. 15, 2019).
[19.4] Panera Bread Foundation, Inc. v. Commissioner (March 24, 2020).

§ 17.5 SELF-DEALING RULES

(e) Incidental and Tenuous Benefits

p. 742. *Insert as first complete paragraph, before heading:*

A private foundation, created and solely funded by a utility providing electricity and natural gas services, proposed to make grants to governmental bodies and other public charities to offset the cost difference between the purchase of gasoline and diesel vehicles and the purchase of electric vehicles. Prospective grantees will include a governmental entity operating a city bus system and a public university. Essentially, the purpose of these grants is to subsidize the purchase of electric buses for the city. The self-dealing rules were implicated, inasmuch as the utility is a disqualified person with respect to the foundation (being a substantial contributor). The potential problem was that the purchase of the electric vehicles will result in additional sales of electricity by the utility. The IRS dismissed this issue, however, holding that the additional sales "will be negligible in comparison with [the] utility's total electricity sales and minimal in relation to the [amount of the] proposed grants."[63.1]

§ 17.6 OTHER PRIVATE FOUNDATIONS RULES

(d) Taxable Expenditures Rules

pp. 744–745. *Delete last paragraph on p. 744 and carryover text on p. 745, including footnotes.*

[63.1]Priv. Ltr. Rul. 202034001. It appears that this charitable organization need not be a private foundation. Inasmuch as the entity being benefited is a governmental body, it could be a supporting organization (see § 15.7) and avoid the self-dealing rules.

Table of Cases

Stark v. Commissioner, § 14.7(b)

Steele v. Commissioner, § 2.8(g)

Swaggart Ministries v. Board of Equal-
ization of California, § 2.5(g)

Texas et al. v. United States, § 1.9(b)

Texas Learning Technology Group v.
Commissioner, § 15.3(g)

Texas Monthly, Inc. v. Bullock, § 2.5(g)

Thorne v. Commissioner, §§ 8.1(a),
8.5(c)

Todd v. Commissioner, § 14.4(b)

Triumph Mixed Use Investments LLC v.
Commissioner, § 14.1

Trust U/W of Bella Mabury v. Commissioner, §§ 6.7(c), 15.7(a)

Trust U/W Emily Oblinger v. Commissioner, § 11.2(b)

Trustees for the Home for Aged Women
v. United States, § 15.4(b)

Trustees of the Louise Home v. Commissioner, § 10.1

Underwood v. United States, §§ 5.8(g),
9.9

Unified Control Systems, Inc., *In re*, §§
1.9, 5.15

United Cancer Council, Inc. v. Commissioner, §§ 5.1, 5.2

United Libertarian Fellowship, Inc. v.
Commissioner, § 2.5(d)

United States v. American Bar Endowment, §§ 14.1, 16.2

United States v. Feinblatt, § 1.9(b)

United States v. Feinblatt (*In re* Kline), §
1.10

United States v. Kahriger, § 1.9(b)

United States v. Reorganized CF&I Fabricators of Utah, Inc., § 1.9(b)

United States v. Sanchez, § 1.9(b)

United States Bankruptcy Court of Central District of California re Mol-
nick's Inc., § 1.10

U.S. House of Representatives v. Texas,
§ 1.9(b)

Variety Club Tent No. 6 Charities, Inc.
v. Commissioner, § 5.1

Vigilant Hose Company of Emmitsburg
v. United States, § 11.1(b)

Villareale v. Commissioner, § 14.9(b)

Warren M. Goodspeed Scholarship
Fund v. Commissioner, §§ 15.7(c),
15.7(i)

Wayne Baseball, Inc. v. Commissioner, §
1.7

Wasie v. Commissioner, §§ 5.4, 5.6(g)

Wendell Falls Development, LLC v.
Commissioner, § 14.1

West Virginia State Medical Association
v. Commissioner, § 11.1(b)

Westward Ho v. Commissioner, §§ 1.7,
9.3(c)

White's Iowa Manual Labor Institute v.
Commissioner, § 11.2(b)

William F., Mable E., and Margaret K.
Quarrie Charitable Fund v. Commissioner, § 15.7(c)

Williams Home, Inc. v. United States, §§
10.0, 15.4(b)

William Wikoff Smith Trust Estate, "The
W.W. Smith Foundation," § 1.8

Table of IRS Revenue Rulings and Revenue Procedures

Revenue Rulings	Section(s)	Revenue Rulings	Section(s)
56-304	9.3(e)	71-460	6.5(f)
56-403	1.7	72-101	5.2, 15.3(b)
56-437	5.4	72-244	3.9
57-128	15.3(g)	72-369	11.3(d)
59-60	5.6(d)	72-430	15.3(b)
62-23	15.3(b)	72-625	6.8
63-252	9.6	73-235	6.8
64-104	10.3(c)	73-256	9.3
64-128	15.3(b)	73-320	3.1(d), 6.8, 10.3(b)
66-79	2.5(b), 9.6	73-363	5.4(c)
66-97	10.3(b)	73-407	5.8(d), 17.5(e)
66-104	17.5(d)	73-434	15.3(b)
66-177	3.9	73-455	4.1
66-358	5.8(d), 17.5(e)	73-543	15.3(b)
67-5	6.1	73-546	5.6(g)
67-8	1.7	73-595	5.6(g)
67-72	5.2	73-601	5.6(a)
67-106	6.7(c)	73-613	5.6(f)
67-108	6.7(c)	74-125	9.3(c)
67-149	1.3	74-183	3.9, 10.5
67-325	1.7	74-224	15.3(a)
68-14	5.2	74-229	15.7
68-16	9.9	74-238	6.8
68-117	6.5(f)	74-287	4.2, 5.11, 17.4
68-145	10.3(c)	74-315	6.4(b)
68-165	6.5(f)	74-316	8.1(a)
68-175	15.3(b)	74-368	1.9
68-373	11.2(c)	74-405	5.7
68-432	5.8(e)	74-450	3.1(a), 6.5(e)
68-504	5.2	74-490	13.3
68-601	5.12(c)	74-497	10.3(b)
68-658	5.8(d)	74-498	6.2(c)
69-492	15.3(b)	74-540	9.3
69-528	11.1(b)	74-560	6.5(c)
69-545	2.8(e)	74-572	15.3(c)
70-47	5.8(e)	74-579	10.4, 10.4(b)
70-186	5.2	74-591	5.6(c), 5.6(f)
70-270	1.8	74-600	5.4(c), 5.8(g)
70-344	10.3(b)	74-601	5.1
70-585	2.5(b)	74-614	9.8(a)
71-20	9.4, 12.3(d)	75-25	5.14, 7.2(a)

Revenue Rulings	Section(s)	Revenue Rulings	Section(s)
75-38	1.8	77-7	6.5(a)
75-42	5.8(d)	77-17	10.3(b)
75-65	9.6	77-44	9.3, 9.3(c)
75-196	5.2	77-74	6.7(e)
75-207	6.2(c)	77-113	13.4
75-215	15.3(b)	77-114	2.6
75-270	6.8	77-116	15.4(b), 15.6(c)
75-282	15.7(j)	77-160	5.8(b), 5.8(e)
75-286	5.2	77-161	9.9
75-289	13.3	77-208	15.4(b)
75-290	2.6	77-212	9.3(h)
75-335	5.8(d)	77-213	9.6(h)
75-336	10.3(d)	77-225	16.2
75-359	15.3(g)	77-246	9.8(c)
75-387	15.5(d), 15.6(c)	77-251	5.10
75-391	5.15(d)	77-252	6.8
75-393	9.3(b)	77-255	15.4(a)
75-410	10.4(a)	77-259	5.4, 5.6(g)
75-435	9.6, 15.4(a)	77-287	6.3(e)
75-436	15.7(i)	77-288	5.6(g)
75-437	15.7(i)	77-289	3.9
75-442	3.1(d), 6.8	77-331	5.8(d)
75-443	6.8	77-367	5.8(d), 17.5(e)
75-492	15.3(b)	77-379	5.4(b)
75-495	6.5(c)	77-380	9.3(a), 9.3(b)
75-511	6.5(e)	77-434	9.3(b)
76-10	5.4(d)	77-469	15.4(b)
76-18	5.4(a)	77-473	4.8
76-22	9.8(c)	78-41	15.7(j)
76-85	6.2(c), 7.3	78-45	6.5(a)
76-92	3.7, 13.4	78-76	5.15(d)
76-158	5.11(b)	78-77	5.4
76-159	5.10	78-82	15.3(b)
76-167	15.3(b)	78-88	11.4(a)
76-193	6.8	78-90	8.3
76-248	3.1(d), 6.8, 10.4(a)	78-95	15.4(a)
76-330	3.9	78-102	6.5(c)
76-340	9.3(d), 9.3(e)	78-144	6.2(c)
76-384	15.3(b)	78-148	6.5(e)
76-401	15.9	78-309	15.3(b)
76-416	15.4(a)	78-315	3.1(b)
76-417	15.3(b)	78-367	6.3(e)
76-440	15.4(b), 15.5(c)	78-386	13.4
76-448	4.9	78-387	13.5(b)
76-452	15.3(c)	78-395	5.4, 5.5(a)
76-459	5.4(d)	78-426	11.2(c)
76-460	9.3(b)	78-428	9.8(c)
76-461	9.3(a), 9.3(b)	79-18	2.5(b)

Revenue Rulings	Section(s)
79-130	15.3(b)
79-131	9.3(e)
79-197	15.7(c)
79-200	10.4(a)
79-319	6.5(a)
79-340	10.3(c)
79-365	9.3(e)
79-374	5.4(d)
79-375	6.5(a)
80-69	14.3
80-97	9.9
80-108	2.6
80-118	10.3(c)
80-132	5.5(a)
80-133	2.4(d), 8.1(a)
80-207	4.9, 6.5(b), 15.7(i)
80-233	14.3
80-259	2.6
80-301	1.7
80-302	1.7
80-305	3.4, 15.7(i)
80-310	5.8(d), 17.5(e)
81-29	9.8(a)
81-40	5.4(b), 5.15(a)
81-43	15.7(c)
81-46	9.3(g)
81-61	2.5(b)
81-76	4.3
81-111	7.1(d)
81-125	9.4(b), 9.7(a)
81-217	9.3(e)
81-276	15.4(b)
81-307	16.2
82-132	15.4(b)
82-136	5.8(d)
82-137	3.1(e), 6.2(d)
82-223	5.7, 9.9
83-153	15.4(b), 15.5(d), 15.6(c)
84-169	10.0, 10.5
85-162	5.8(d)
85-175	9.3(d)
86-53	5.14
86-63	14.1
86-77	9.3(g)
86-90	9.3(e)
89-64	5.12(c)
92-59	2.8(e)
93-84	10.3(b)

Revenue Rulings	Section(s)
95-8	11.4(a)
98-15	5.2
2002-28	13.1, 13.5, 13.5(a)
2002-43	5.5
2003-12	12.3(e)
2003-13	10.2(c), 13.1, 13.3, 13.3(c)
2003-32	9.3(e)
2007-41	9.1(c), 9.8(d)
2008-41	5.3, 5.13
2009-9	8.4(a)
2011-9	10.3(b)

Revenue Procedures	Section(s)
76-47	9.3(e)
77-20	15.4(d)
80-27	9.10A
80-39	9.3(e)
81-46	12.3(d)
81-65	9.3(e)
82-2	2.1
83-32	3.7
83-36	9.3(e)
84-47	2.6
85-51	9.3(e)
92-59	2.8(e)
92-75	2.7(b)
92-85	2.6
92-94	6.5(f), 9.7(a)
93-28	2.6
94-17	3.9
94-78	9.3(e)
96-32	7.3
98-25	9.4, 12.3(d)
2002-9	10.4(c)
2007-52	2.6
2009-20	5.11, 8.4(a)
2011-36	12.0
2017-53	9.6
2018-15	2.5
2018-32	9.4(c), 15.11
2020-1	2.7(a), 2.7(b)
2020-2	2.7(a)

Revenue Procedures	Section(s)
2020-3	5.12(c)
2020-5	2.5, 2.5(b), 2.5(c), 2.5(d), 2.6, 2.7, 2.7(a), 3.1(h), 9.2(c), 9.3(g), 13.1, 13.3(c), 13.4, 15.2, 15.5(c), 15.8(d)
2020-8	2.5(a)

Table of IRS Private Determinations Cited in Text

Private Letter Rulings	Section(s)	Private Letter Rulings	Section(s)
7751033	5.4(e)	8623080	5.0
7810038	5.4(e)	8627055	6.5(e)
7817081	17.5(e)	8629062	13.5(d)
7821141	6.5(e)	8644003	5.8(d), 17.5(e)
7823072	6.2(c)	8651087	5.4(d)
7828012	6.5(b)	8713056	6.5(b)
7830122	9.3(g)	8717024	9.7(j)
7847049	5.14, 10.3(d)	8718006	8.1(a)
7851096	9.3(d)	8719004	5.8(c)
7933084	6.3(e)	8719038	15.7(j)
7952117	17.5(a)	8721107	11.4(a)
8001046	10.3(d)	8723001	5.4(b)
8004086	17.5(e)	8730061	10.3(b)
8038049	5.4(b), 5.4(f)	8750006	6.5(a)
8047007	10.4(a)	8802008	10.4(b)
8128072	5.8(b)	8807002	9.3(e)
8202082	5.7	8812046	6.5(b)
8210120	15.7(j)	8822096	15.4(a), 15.5(d)
8214023	10.3(b)	8824001	5.4(c)
8220101	3.8	8824010	5.9(b)
8226127	15.7(j)	8825116	15.7
8226159	5.8(d)	8826029	9.3(h)
8232051	6.5(b)	8830070	6.5(e)
8234149	5.4	8832074	8.3
8315060	6.2(b)	8839003	6.5(a)
8331082	5.9(b)	8840055	7.1(b)
8407095	7.1(b), 7.1(d)	8842045	5.4(e)
8409039	5.5(a)	8906062	6.5(c)
8425080	17.5(f)	8909066	10.3(g)
8449069	10.3(d)	8911063	5.10
8502040	5.4	8927031	7.3
8503098	5.7	8929087	5.12(c)
8508097	4.8	8930047	7.3
8508114	7.2(d)	8935061	1.7
8510068	15.5(c)	8942054	5.11
8518067	2.6	8944007	5.8(a)
8525075	4.3	8948034	5.4(d)
8533099	4.8	9008001	5.6(c)
8606040	6.5(b)	9011050	5.6(a), 5.6(e)
		9014004	16.5

TABLE OF IRS PRIVATE DETERMINATIONS CITED IN TEXT

Private Letter Rulings	Section(s)	Private Letter Rulings	Section(s)
9011050	5.6(a)	9316051	1.7
9016003	5.8(a)	9320016	14.5
9018033	3.1(h)	9325061	5.6(a)
9019064	5.9(b)	9327082	5.4(c)
9021066	5.8(f), 17.5(c)	9331046	9.7(a)
9029067	7.2(d)	9333051	7.1(d)
9047001	5.4(a)	9341008	10.3(b)
9050030	9.7(a)	9343033	5.5
9108001	3.1(h)	9347041	6.3(f)
9114025	5.8(a)	9401031	11.2(b)
9114036	5.6(a)	9417018	5.5
9115061	7.2(d)	9426040	15.7(j)
9116032	6.5(c), 6.7(a), 9.3(a)	9434041	15.7(b)
9117070	7.1(d)	9438013	15.7(b)
9124061	7.1(d)	9440033	5.7(c), 9.9
9129006	6.5(e)	9442025	15.7(b)
9129040	9.6	9451067	8.1(a)
9130002	5.1	9503023	5.6(a)
9147008	11.1(c)	9504027	14.5
9203004	3.1(c)	9509042	3.1(f)
9203040	15.4(a)	9510073	5.10
9222052	5.5	9516047	1.7, 5.8(d), 9.3(b)
9222057	5.12(a)	9524033	6.5(e)
9226067	5.9(b)	9530032	5.5, 5.6(b), 5.15(b), 5.15(d)
9233031	6.3(d)	9540042	5.8(b)
9237020	10.3(c)	9551037	6.5(b)
9237032	5.5(f)	9601048	5.15(a)
9237035	5.6(a), 5.6(e), 8.1(a)	9603019	11.4(b)
9238027	5.6(a)	9604006	5.8(d)
9241064	11.4(a)	9608039	15.4(b), 15.5
9242042	5.12(a)	9610032	5.8(b)
9246028	5.12(a)	9614002	5.8(d), 8.1(b)
9247018	14.5	9615030	5.2
9247036	6.5(c)	9619027	5.8(d)
9250039	7.2(b)	9619068	11.2
9252028	11.2, 11.3(a)	9619069	11.2
9252031	9.3(c)	9631004	9.3(d)
9252042	5.12(a)	9637051	15.7(k)
9301022	6.5(e)	9643039	15.7(j)
9301024	11.2(b)	9644063	11.4(a)
9305026	15.7(k)	9645017	15.7(k)
9306034	9.7(a)	9651037	5.4(f)
9307025	5.12(a)	9702003	11.2(b)
9307026	5.6(e), 5.9(b)	9702036	5.6(a)
9308045	5.12(a)	9702040	6.5(c)
9312022	5.9(b), 17.5(b)	9703020	5.8(b)
9316032	11.1(e)		

Private Letter Rulings	Section(s)	Private Letter Rulings	Section(s)
9703031	5.6(a)	200014040	5.4(c), 5.4(e), 5.9(b)
9715031	15.7(j)	200019044	9.6, 9.7(a)
9719041	5.7(c)	200020060	5.4(b), 5.6(b)
9723046	9.8(a)	200028014	12.2(k)
9723047	3.1(b)	200030027	11.1(c)
9724005	10.3(g)	200031053	6.5(f)
9726006	5.8(c)	200033049	11.1(b)
9732031	5.9(b)	200034037	8.3
9741047	1.7	200037053	16.7
9742006	3.7, 3.8	200038049	15.7(j)
9804040	4.8	200041037	6.5
9805021	5.4(d)	200043050	6.5(e)
9807030	6.5(a), 15.4(d), 16.3, 16.14	200043051	3.7
9816030	5.3(c)	200103079	13.3(c)
9818009	10.3(c)	200112022	14.5
9819045	5.8(d)	200112064	5.5(b)
9825004	1.9, 9.3(e)	200114040	5.2
9834033	6.5(c)	200115038	12.2(k)
9838028	10.3(c)	200116047	5.6(a)
9839036	6.5(f)	200117042	5.12(a), 5.12(c)
9844031	5.4(e)	200119061	11.1(e)
9851052	11.1(c)	200123072	5.8(c)
9852023	7.2(d), 8.1(a), 10.3(i)	200124010	5.13
9927047	9.3(b)	200128059	11.1(d)
199905039	6.5(e)	200129041	5.8(d)
199906053	6.5(e)	200132037	5.12(a)
199907028	6.5(e)	200135047	5.6(a)
199910066	8.3	200136026	8.3
199911054	5.3(c)	200136029	6.2(c), 6.5(c)
199913040	5.4(d)	200148071	5.8(d)
199913042	9.8(a)	200149040	5.4(e)
199914040	1.7, 5.8(d), 9.3(b), 9.9	200149045	16.4, 16.14
199915053	14.5	200150039	16.7
199925029	14.5	200202077	7.3
199927046	5.6(a)	200204040	15.4(d)
199939046	7.1(c)	200208039	5.13, 13.0
199939049	5.8(d)	200209061	9.3(h)
199943044	3.1(b), 8.3	200210029	11.1(e)
199943047	4.9	200217056	5.6(a)
199943058	3.1(b), 8.3	200218036	5.12(c)
199950039	5.4(c), 5.8(d)	200224035	10.6
199952086	11.3(a)	200225037	5.12(a)
199952092	9.7(c)	200228026	5.6(a)
200007039	5.6(a)	200232036	5.5(b)
200009053	9.3(d)	200235042	11.4(a)
200010061	11.4(a)	200238053	5.6(a)

Private Letter Rulings	Section(s)	Private Letter Rulings	Section(s)
200252092	5.3	200517031	5.4(f)
200303062	11.2(e)	200525014	5.13
200304025	5.13	200527020	5.4(d)
200307084	5.8(d)	200529004	12.3(e)
200309027	5.8(d)	200532058	7.1(a)
200310024	5.13	200536027	5.9(b)
200311033	3.3	200542037	4.8
200315031	5.6(a)	200548026	6.3(e), 6.3(f)
200316042	5.8(d)	200551025	5.4(f)
200318069	8.1(a)	200603029	9.3(d)
200324056	5.6(a)	200603031	8.3
200324057	9.4, 12.3(d)	200604034	4.8
200326039	5.6(a)	200605014	4.8, 5.8(d)
200327060	9.3(b)	200606042	5.2
200327062	6.5(e)	200607027	13.5
200328049	6.5(e)	200610020	8.3
200329049	6.2(e), 6.2(f)	200611034	7.1(c)
200331005	8.3	200614030	15.7(b)
200332018	5.2	200614032	5.13
200332020	7.2(d)	200620029	5.8(d)
200333030	5.2	200620030	5.11
200335037	5.8(c)	200620036	13.4
200343026	5.6(a)	200621032	8.1(a)
200343027	7.3, 8.3	200623068	13.4
200347014	8.3	200625035	11.2(d)
200347017	7.3	200634016	7.2(b)
200347018	6.5(e)	200635018	5.2
200349007	9.3(b)	200637041	8.1(a)
200350022	5.4	200644050	10.2(a)
200408033	9.3(c)	200649030	5.7(a)
200414050	6.2(c)	200702031	6.3(d), 14.5
200420029	5.4(f)	200703037	11.1(b)
200421010	5.9(b), 13.5	200709065	7.3
200425051	5.8(d)	200714025	3.8
200431018	3.1(a), 6.5(d)	200725043	6.5(c)
200432026	11.4(b)	200727018	5.6(g)
200433028	8.2	200727019	5.11
200434026	6.5(e)	200727021	15.3(a)
200434028	7.3	200728044	11.1(e)
200437036	15.5(c)	200731034	15.7(c)
200438042	7.2(d)	200736037	2.8(g), 5.3
200443045	5.5(b), 5.8(d), 5.11	200737044	2.8(g)
200445023	16.3	200750020	4.5, 5.11(c)
200501021	5.6(a), 5.6(g)	200810025	15.7(m)
200508018	15.5(a)	200825050	7.3
200515021	15.4(a), 15.4(b)	200828029	2.8(g)
		200831029	5.8(g)

Private Letter Rulings	Section(s)	Private Letter Rulings	Section(s)
200832027	11.3(d)	201311035	7.6, 16.9
200839034	9.3(b)	201315031	6.2(c)
200842050	17.4	201316021	5.12(a)
200844022	15.7(m)	201321024	13.5
200846041	10.5, 15.2	201329027	7.2(d)
200850046	5.8(g)	201321027	5.12(a)
200852050	7.3	201322046	15.4(d)
200903081	15.7(b)	201323029	6.2(c), 7.3
200916035	2.8(g)	201325017	2.8(g)
200926033	7.2(b)	201332013	2.8(g)
200926049	15.3(a)	201335020	6.5(a)
200937038	6.5(b)	201336019	6.5(a)
200944055	5.6(c)	201338059	15.9
201004046	15.7(m)	201346011	5.4(d), 5.4(e)
201006032	7.3	201403016	15.4(d)
201007076	15.7(m)	201407021	5.11, 5.11(b)
201012050	5.4	201414031	7.2(a)
201013065	13.5(d)	201415010	5.3(b), 5.4(d)
201013066	13.5(d)	201417022	17.5(e)
201021029	1.9	201419017	6.2(c)
201022030	9.3(d)	201421022	2.8(g)
201029039	5.8(d)	201421023	5.8(b)
201029040	6.5	201422027	7.1(b)
201044025	5.2	201423032	5.4(e)
201052022	15.7(m)	201430017	7.1(a), 8.1(a)
201113041	2.8(g)	201432025	5.8(g)
201115030	15.7(m)	201433021	4.0
201129049	5.12(c)	201435016	13.5
201130006	13.5	201436050	2.8(g)
201130008	4.9	201436051	17.3
201134023	6.5(d)	201437014	6.5(a)
201143022	9.7(a)	201440023	5.2
201145027	8.3	201441018	10.3(a)
201152021	6.5(e)	201442061	8.3
201203025	2.8(g)	201442066	5.2
201209011	2.8(g)	201448023	5.12(a)
201221022	15.3(a)	201507024	15.5(c)
201221024	9.3(b)	201510050	4.4
201232034	15.3(a)	201512004	15.5(c)
201239011	15.5(c)	201516069	15.5(c)
201242014	2.8(g), 15.3(a)	201525008	17.5(e)
201246037	15.3(a)	201525014	2.8(g)
201252021	2.8(g)	201534018	6.5(e)
201301015	5.8(c)	201540019	5.2
201302040	2.8(g)	201541011	9.3(a)
201307008	15.4(d)	201541013	2.8(g)

Private Letter Rulings	Section(s)
201603032	7.3, 11.3(b)
201610022	9.3(a)
201617012	5.2
201624001	5.14
201626004	11.2
201627005	6.5(e)
201636021	7.2(d)
201640022	5.1
201641023	5.1
201642001	5.11(c)
201645011	7.4
201652004	9.5
201701002	11.3(e)
201703003	1.9, 1.9(a), 5.3(a), 5.11(c)
201710005	7.3
201711014	15.5(c)
201713002	3.8
201714031	5.8(d), 17.5(e)
201718002	5.4, 5.8(d), 17.5(e)
201719004	5.11, 6.5(a)
201723005	5.11
201724001	9.5
201730012	4.4
201731019	5.1
201737003	7.2(c), 10.5
201740002	11.4(a)
201745001	5.8(c), 9.9
201801014	1.8(g), 5.8(d), 17.5(f)
201808010	3.9, 10.5
201820019	5.6(e)
201821005	3.1(c), 8.3
201825004	15.7(g)
201829003	6.2(c)
201830003	9.9
201831007	3.3
201835014	6.5(e)
201844013	15.9
201848005	14.5
201849009	5.11, 5.12(a), 11.3(f), 11.4(a)
201850012	5.12(c)
201850023	15.5(c)
201851003	9.9
201907004	5.5, 5.11(b)
201909015	15.5(c)
201911010	17.3A
201918020	5.1
201919018	9.3(d)

Private Letter Rulings	Section(s)
201922038	16.12
201923027	15.5(c)
201930017	13.6
201937003	5.6(a)
201940013	9.11(b)
201945030	9.3(a)
201947020	3.9
201952009	15.5(c)
202017035	15.9
202034001	17.5(e)

Technical Advice Memoranda	Section(s)
7734022	5.9(b)
8106008	5.12(c)
8449008	17.5(c)
8719004	5.5(a), 5.8(c)
8723001	5.8(b)
8836033	16.3
9221002	5.4(c)
9240001	9.8
9335001	5.1
9404032	5.6(a)
9408006	5.15(e)
9424004	1.9, 7.7
9509002	11.2(a)
9609007	9.2(a)
9627001	5.8
9645004	11.1(b)
9646002	5.4(d), 5.15(f)
9702004	11.1(b)
9724005	10.3(b)
9822006	11.2(b)
9825001	5.8
9853001	11.2(b)
9901002	11.2(b)
200047048	15.4(b)
200047049	11.1(e)
200151045	2.5(b)
200218037	2.5(b)
200218038	8.1, 8.1(a)
200307084	5.8(d)
200347023	6.7(d), 7.6, 8.5, 9.11(b)
200437040	15.3(a)

TABLE OF IRS PRIVATE DETERMINATIONS CITED IN TEXT

Technical Advice Memoranda	Section(s)
200452037	9.11(b)
200613038	10.2(c)
200727019	5.11, 5.11(c)
201129050	6.7(d), 9.11(b)
201151028	5.2
201351027	9.11(b)
201407024	15.3(b)
201441021	7.7
201447007	9.11
201448032	7.7
201821005	3.1(c)
201837014	7.3

General Counsel Memoranda	Section(s)
39442	3.1(a)
39445	4.6, 5.11
39508	15.7(j)
39632	5.8(c)
39741	5.8(g)
39748	15.4(a), 15.6(c), 16.7
39770	5.4(e)
39808	6.4(a), 6.7(a)
39862	5.1
39875	15.4(a), 15.6(c), 16.7
39876	1.7

General Counsel Memoranda	Section(s)
34369	11.1(b)
35554	10.4(b)
37485	15.2
38437	15.3(b)
38459	5.1
38840	2.5, 3.9
39066	5.15(d)
39104	15.5(d)
39107	5.8(c)
39195	7.1(d)

Table of IRS Private Letter Rulings, Technical Advice Memoranda, and General Counsel Memoranda

The following citations, to pronouncements from the Internal Revenue Service issued in the context of specific cases, are coordinated to the footnotes of the appropriate chapters.

Citations are to IRS private letter rulings, technical advice memoranda, and general counsel memoranda, other than those specifically referenced in footnotes, directly pertinent to the material discussed in the text. Nine-number or seven-number items are either private letter rulings or technical advice memoranda; five-number items are general counsel memoranda.

These pronouncements are not to be cited as precedent (IRC § 6110(k)(3)) but are useful in illuminating the position of the IRS on the subjects involved.

Chapter One	Introduction to Private Foundations
13	39562
89	9110042, 9226055, 9329041, 9736047
110	200243050

Chapter Three	Types of Private Foundations
2	8628080, 8819002, 8927030, 9108001, 9137049, 9203004, 9411009, 9646002
32.1	201821005
53	8845059
57	9108001
65	8934042, 9509042
86	9746058
93	9611047, 201625003
101.1	201831007
123	9726009, 9730002
139	200223008
145	8628050, 8631024, 8643087, 8644014, 8644069, 8649057, 8808031, 9201037, 9647023, 200004052
149	201831009
151	8846058
154	8709050
163	8645058, 9210005, 9407006
167	8718042
171	201831009
172	200223008
182	39842
191	39842
193	201737003

Chapter Four	Disqualified Persons
2	201433022–201433024
4	9031028
20	8735033, 9426044
21	8735033, 8823050, 9013019, 9015072, 9016003, 9018032, 9019075, 9033054, 9033055, 9051009, 9415011, 9421039, 9513029, 9533020, 9626029, 9823050, 9850019, 199939046, 199952092, 200220030, 200225045, 200226045
22	8933059, 9041003, 9041061, 9052025, 9052027, 9415011
26	8950037
27	8802001, 9530072
29	201407023
36	8950036, 9442040, 201441018
41	8909027, 8944007, 9015055
60	200813043
62	201730017, 201730018
68	8650090
70	8626098
73	199939046
80	8940074
93	9031028

Chapter Five	Self-Dealing
6	8810096, 8846005, 8917019, 9108023, 9115056, 9138069, 9426044
8	8922091, 9512018, 9623018
56	200332019
60	200324035, 200403051
63	9844031, 199943057, 200018062, 200124024, 200711023
70	9008001
71	201624013
72	8912061, 9350038, 9525056, 9527034, 9546020
74	9623018
75	199924069, 200003051
79	200310024
79.1	202016002–202016006
81	8622056, 8630053, 8727082, 9205001, 200148069
83	8839071, 9019061
85	8945060, 9137006
87	8644001, 9137006, 9235055, 9241064, 9308045, 9323003, 9348052, 9810026–9810029
88	8849059, 9113025, 9119009, 9333050, 9526033, 201012050
90	199952093, 200043047
94	200729043
103	8810005, 8834029, 9014033, 9312022, 200720021
106	8834029, 9751034, 201346011
113	8824001, 39741
114	9732031, 9751034, 9805021, 199913040, 199950039, 201718002

Chapter Five	Self-Dealing
116	8824010, 8909037, 8934054, 9139024
117	9751034, 9810037
120	9810037
122	9641033
123	9114025, 9805021, 200011051
140	9705013, 200318069, 200420029, 200423029
142	200420029
153	8719004, 39632
155	8728050, 9013004, 9013005, 9312024, 9350038, 9724018
162	9831026, 199941053, 200222037
166	8909037
169	201346011
170	8728050, 9234031, 9333050, 9411018, 9411019, 200111051, 200111052, 200112065
180	9008001
181	8628084, 8650092, 8651087, 8726004, 8732064, 8824010, 8948034, 9019064, 9019075, 9226067 (affirmed by 9433027), 9238027, 9238028, 9307026, 9308045, 9343033, 9533041, 9546020, 9703031, 199905025, 200001049, 200007039, 200027055, 200607028, 201346011, 39660
183	9011050, 9013004, 9013005, 9015070, 9015071, 9115056, 9237035, 9325061, 9425004, 9533041, 9626007, 199905025, 199927046, 200303061
186	201221031
191	200050047
192	9301026, 200352021
193	200326040, 200501022
194	199905025, 200303061, 201630009
196	200551025
198	9702037–9702039, 201221031
199	200228027–200228029, 201221031
200	9238028, 200116047, 200228026, 200238053
201	200116047, 200213028, 200217056, 200228026–200228029, 200241048
252	8922068, 9041003, 9041061, 9431054, 9731056
254	8722078, 9001015, 9001016, 9114036, 9351039, 9425004, 9535043, 9619049, 9734038, 9734045–9734050, 200023051, 200727018
260	200501022
261	8732041, 8743085, 8944007, 9139024, 9144038
262	8708029, 8726070, 8920041, 9041003, 9041061, 9101018, 9513029
266	199945056, 199945057
285	8719036, 8947035, 9137006, 9307025, 9408006, 9626007
288	8944007, 9130030, 9533041, 9623018
291	201421024
296	9714010 (revoking 9233053)
298	199905038, 200232036, 200312003 (suspended by 200530007), 200312004
299	200831035
306	8944007, 9431029, 9540042, 9604031, 9614003, 9623018, 9726006, 9740023, 9810026–9810029, 201029039, 201346011, 201435017

Chapter Five	Self-Dealing
307	8918023
308	8644003, 8724056, 8737084, 8738074, 8749041, 8811016, 8842045, 9011053, 9019075, 9021066, 9022056, 9235062, 9304036, 9325046, 9336041, 9448047, 9513017, 9535015 (as modified by 9540063), 9535044, 9547019, 9608039, 9652033
309	8815004
320	200620029
326	199917077 (reversing 9544023), 199917079 (reversing 9314058)
330	200149040
340	9819045, 9826031, 9826032, 200019044, 200222005, 200222034, 200247051, 200423029, 200441033, 200532055, 200551025, 201311034
341	200148072, 200219038
346	9814036–9814038, 9826040, 199926048, 200222037
351	200831030, 200831031
368	8723001, 9210025, 9503023, 39644
383	8911063
384	200225042
385	8819082, 9104035, 9140061, 9204053, 9210029, 9222057, 9222058, 9324030, 9325061 (affirmed (9404032)), 9333050, 9402024, 9411018, 9411019, 9525056
386	8710058, 8718049
392	201407023
394	9009067
412	9047001, 9426044
418	8330110, 8650090, 8724036
419.1	8710095, 9009067, 9421039
421	8728050, 8728076, 8929048, 8929049, 8929087, 8942054, 9042030, 9042040, 9047054, 9108024, 9112012, 9127052, 9210040, 9246028, 9252042, 9308045, 9320041, 9350038, 9421005, 9434042, 9438045, 9501038, 9646031, 9734020, 9739033, 9752071, 9818063, 9839028, 9839029, 199917078, 199930048, 200005027, 200007006, 200024052, 200620031–200620035, 200635015, 200649031, 200649032, 200727019, 201849009
428	8942054
432	9014063, 9818063, 200628038, 200651038, 201446024
436	9210040, 200134033
435.7	200218041, 200218042, 200219036, 200219039, 200227044, 200607023
441	200124029, 200132032, 200148080, 200207028, 200207029, 200218036, 200218041, 200218042, 200219036, 200219039, 200224033, 200225037, 200227044, 200232031, 200232033, 200233031, 200519082, 200532053, 200532054, 200548026, 200620030–200620035, 200628038, 200635015, 200651038, 201016084, 201145026, 201206019, 201441020, 201445017, 201446024, 201448023
460	200441024, 200525014, 200543061, 200725044, 200802032, 200802033, 200814003, 200817039, 200824022, 200809044, 200912036

Chapter Five	Self-Dealing
462	8622056, 8630153, 8642094, 8906013, 9015055, 9040063, 9040064, 9117043, 9146042, 9235050, 933033, 9338046, 9346019, 9347021, 9719039 (superseded and modified by 9723025), 200015007, 200521028
463	8712064, 8724058, 9101021, 9108030, 9108036, 9237032, 9721035, 9731024 (revoking 9374035)
467	9237032
473	8819007, 8927060, 8949081
480	8818012

Chapter Six	Mandatory Distributions
20	8642052, 8650049, 8715046, 8737102, 8752033, 8846005, 8906062, 9035055, 9247037, 9333050, 9338042, 9411009, 9426044, 9739032, 200224035
22	199905038
23	8329041
27	201029040, 202024014
28	200136029
49	8620082, 8724073, 8906062, 8942053, 9236035, 9316046, 9608039, 39561
61	200148078
68	8826010, 9530033, 9604006
69	8909037
70	8650091
99	8715046, 8906062, 8934043, 9117040, 9117044, 9139027, 9304022, 9620039, 9702040
103	8641046, 8647070, 8746079, 8747052, 8812046, 8818002, 8839003, 8909057, 8923071, 9115049, 9117044, 9131046, 9351027, 9426044
118	200937038
119	8803060, 8831006, 9017024, 9211062, 9237043
121	9604006, 9608039, 9702040, 9723047, 9751030, 9834033, 9834083, 199933051, 20000345–20000347, 200010052, 200026028, 200043052, 200207031, 200209061, 200221052, 200225042, 200246036, 200251019, 200252098, 200304035, 200324056, 200332019, 200341024, 200704037, 200706015, 200718033, 200825049, 200947065, 39883
135	8713056–8713058, 8936020, 9646022, 201437015
176	8722079
189	8722079
191	8834011
194	200347021
196	9135058
198	9235063

Chapter Six	Mandatory Distributions
215	8627055, 8709013, 8719040, 8722079, 8723053, 8728079, 8733036, 8750006, 8750068, 8752039, 8753055, 8812077, 8817020, 8824055, 8825061, 8831042, 8846020, 8849025, 8849104, 8850023, 8909010, 8909026, 8909035, 8918046, 8918089, 8926075, 8934013, 8934032, 8935035, 8936049, 8940057, 8941005, 8942098, 9010010, 9012006, 9014044, 9015036, 9015037, 9016057, 9017074, 9018033, 9018067, 9018069, 9018070, 9025084, 9025087, 9025090, 9030059, 9034061, 9115056, 9117067, 9129005, 9129006, 9129055, 9135058, 9144036, 9146039, 9147057, 9148049, 9238040 (extended by 9740031), 9718035, 9730012, 9734007, 9751031, 980958, 9811058, 9814052, 9830021, 9834038, 199905039, 199906052, 199906053, 199907028, 199910066, 199922067, 199926050, 199943051, 199952095, 200001047, 200037049, 200011069, 200020059, 200023050, 200026029, 200028037, 200034036, 200043054, 200048048, 200107041, 200116054, 200118055, 200121077, 200132041, 200134030, 200147057, 200149039, 200150037, 200204037, 200207030, 200212034, 200224031, 200224032, 200225036, 200230040, 200235036, 200241052, 200243054, 200245059, 200247054, 200302051, 200303063, 200311040, 200411049, 200411050, 200418046, 200418053, 200430043, 200441036, 200443044, 200444036, 200512022, 200512024, 200512026, 200513029, 200513031, 200522014, 200522015, 200525015–200525017, 200534024, 200537035, 200542036, 200604035, 200605015, 200621028–200621030, 200628037, 200634037, 200641009, 200641010, 200644040, 200739011, 200915048, 200915050, 200916032, 200926030, 200926032, 201005054, 201005055, 201015033, 201031037, 201047025, 201105049, 201111020, 201122030, 201128033, 201130007, 201131032, 201131033, 201134024, 201134029, 201146019, 201152021, 201210040, 201233019 201449003, 201452021, 201501016, 201503022, 201503023, 201512002, 201522007, 201529014, 201533015, 201533016, 201606033, 201628022, 201641031, 201628022, 201727009, 201727010, 201728024, 201824015, 201833027, 201835013, 201843017, 201848018, 201904017, 201904019, 201905007, 201919017, 202005025, 202005027, 202009030, 202010007, 202011012 , 202017032, 202017036, 202023011, 202025001, 202032005
217	8738040
223	8629058
232	9629020
237	9651038
238	9651038, 9839036, 200010056
253	8728003
254	201231016
255	9742037, 9752066
257	9015072, 9041003, 9041061, 9306035, 39808
294	200246031

Chapter Seven	Excess Business Holdings
4	8708052, 9651037
12	8932042, 9001015, 9001016, 9010025, 9412039, 9823058, 9844033, 200018062, 200444042, 200448049–200448051, 200450036, 200551025, 200517031, 200548026, 200611034, 200635015, 200715015, 201127011, 201407023, 201422027, 201430017, 201435017, 201447043, 201630009, 201723006
46	8822055, 8920012, 9250039, 9325046, 9432019, 9551034
48	201303021
56	8649080, 200134026
58	201338043
59	8718042
61	9117070
63	9124061, 9340002, 9507020, 39855
72	8642071, 8949081, 9308046
73	8830084, 8920086, 9016003, 9308046, 9432019
90	8929048, 8929049, 8929087, 8932090, 8942070, 8950036, 9047054, 9250039, 9752074, 9852023, 200011051, 200024052, 200117042, 200846038, 201441018, 201510055, 201510056, 201849009
93	9047054, 9242016
105	8737085, 9029067, 9115061, 9211067, 9528006, 9608007, 9646031, 9709005, 9814044, 200040036, 200040037, 200241047, 200332020, 200407024, 200524030, 200526021, 200552018, 200650018, 200833018, 200951038, 201007062, 201007066, 201105053, 201220037, 201228039, 201229011, 201232038, 201636021
108	200438043
109	199923057
111	8842067, 8927031, 8930047, 8942070, 8943022, 9308045, 9320052, 9550138, 9551037, 199950039
128	201021045
129	200822041
145	8724058

Chapter Eight	Jeopardizing Investments
4	8631004, 9205001, 39537
6	200218038
7	8718006, 9237035
9	8711001, 8909037
21	9723045
22	9626029, 9852023
24	201630009
55	8708067, 8710076
58	8923070, 8923071, 8943022
71	200331006–200331008
76	8728053, 8733043, 8807048, 8810026, 8821087, 9033063, 9111035, 9112013, 9131046, 9134030, 9134031, 9134033, 9148049, 9148052, 9426044, 9434031, 9551005, 9608039, 9826048, 199910066, 199943044, 199947038, 199950039, 200603031, 39720

Chapter Nine	Taxable Expenditures
35	8823050, 9240001, 39883
59	200203069
64	9719041
83	201449006
84	8642063, 9751029, 201621016
88	8642063, 8822056, 8822080, 9540044, 9629025, 9640021, 9825004
92	8734068
94	200419035
95	9835043, 9840052
101	8721076, 9151040
118	200041033, 200123073
121	9425035
124	8908042, 200031053
130	8814033, 8825060, 8830027, 8830057, 8830058, 8925070, 9012018–9012022, 9015026, 9015066, 9017078, 9030061, 9033065, 9043051
138	200116045, 200117046
140	9018061, 9036016, 9546027, 201404015
144	8838007, 9138068
147	8838007, 8941046, 9009001, 9235002
157	9130030, 9130037, 9135055, 9135056, 9136029, 9138068, 9139028, 9203042, 9308044, 9308048, 9312034, 9652027, 9652034, 9707021
158	199917077 (reversing 9544023), 199917079 (reversing 9314058)
159	7903003, 8323901, 8626103, 8628078, 8630058, 8641079, 8651092, 8738076, 8738079, 8743101, 8746039, 8746043, 8805007–8805009, 8807002, 8816077, 8816078, 8817050, 8817058, 8817059, 8818042, 8825090, 8825091, 8830056, 8830081, 8837086, 8840007, 8840008, 8844050, 8906011, 8915002, 8924028, 8924060, 8936051, 8941014, 8943002, 9007041, 9022035, 9023040, 9029032, 9033060, 9033064, 9034050, 9036017, 9040058, 9043051, 9044070, 9130037, 9136029, 9138068, 9139028, 9148044, 9204049, 9228045, 9246034, 9329022, 9329037, 9343035, 9344037, 9349025, 9402030, 9403027, 9403028, 9408001, 9417020, 9417026, 9417035, 9418023, 9418032, 9425033, 9425034, 9425036, 9426026, 9444051, 9502010, 9514029, 9517047, 9517048, 9530015, 9530019, 9530035, 9531033, 9541031, 9544043 (amended by 199914056), 9545012, 9548035, 9549033, 9552020, 9603010, 9621045, 9623034, 9627013, 9636027, 9636028, 9638041, 9638045, 9640031, 9647036, 9647038, 9647039, 9651006, 9652032, 9751016, 9752076, 9811056, 9826053, 9835046, 9851048, 199945056, 200005038, 200028043, 200131030, 200131031, 200115041, 200122049, 200135046, 200148056, 200148064, 200224030, 200230041, 200235037, 200420031, 200420032, 200644034, 200644035, 200720020, 200906058, 200907039, 200907041, 200907044, 200907045, 200908047, 200908048, 200909071, 200910059, 200911036, 200911038, 200911039, 200911041, 200912033–200912035, 200912037, 200913064, 200913066, 200915052, 200916033, 200916034, 200917043–200917046, 200918022, 200918023, 200919058–200919060, 200926029,

Chapter Nine	Taxable Expenditures
	200926031, 200926034, 200926035, 200926038, 200926043–200926048, 200931060, 200938031–200938033, 200939031, 200940032, 200943040, 200943041, 200944054, 200945073–200945075, 200950045, 200950046, 200950048, 200950050, 200951036, 201002045, 201002046, 201003021, 201003025, 201006033, 201009014, 201010029, 201014069–201014072, 201015034–201015036, 201016087, 201016091, 201020023, 201020024, 201021028, 201021044, 201023066, 201024067, 201026037, 201027059, 201027060, 201028043, 201028045, 39532
166	199927047
167	8838007, 9015066, 9651036
170	200522016
181	8019043, 8703064, 8717047, 8722001, 8722092, 8723072, 8732028, 8734058, 8738084, 8739059, 8742084, 8912001, 8924045–8924049, 8924069, 8924070, 8925070, 8926006–8926009, 8927030, 8929010, 8932009, 8932043, 8934041, 8941046, 9010009, 9033064, 9033065, 9045013, 9045041, 9116032, 9125041, 9135055, 9135056, 9201038, 9203042, 9632024, 9709007, 9714032, 9719040, 9728035, 9728039, 9728041, 9728042, 9731037, 9751015, 9752032, 9803026, 9809060, 9821058, 9826054, 9830027, 9835043, 9835048, 9838008, 9838009, 9840052, 9844010, 9844011, 9845030, 9850018, 9851048, 9853058, 199901030, 199906053, 199906056, 199914050, 199915060, 199917080, 199919063, 199920042, 199921055, 199925046, 199926051, 199930047, 199930049, 199936050, 199937051, 199938043–199938048, 199939047, 199943043, 200001049, 200026031, 200034034, 200041033, 200043048, 200103080, 200103081, 200116045, 200117046, 200123073, 200148058–200148063, 200148070, 200150029, 200151048, 200217057, 200221052, 200227039, 200228034, 200233026, 200238048, 200238054, 200244020, 200244022, 200247056, 200249010, 200249015, 200250038, 200302047, 200304035, 200305033, 200340026, 200344026–200344028, 200409040, 200419035, 200444037, 200444038, 200444039, 200445045, 200503030, 200517033, 200518080, 200527017, 200527018, 200527022, 200532050, 200533024, 200539028, 200540017 (suspended by 200650026), 200603029, 200607026, 200641011, 200644049, 200842043, 200843044, 200844032, 200844033, 200850034, 200850045, 200851038, 200851039, 200852035, 200852038, 200852039, 200902014, 200903096–200903102, 200905032, 200906058, 200907039, 200907041, 200907044, 200907045, 200908047, 200908048, 200909071, 200910059, 200911036, 200911038, 200911039, 200911041, 200912033–200912035, 200912037, 200913064, 200913066, 200915049, 200915051, 200915052, 200916033, 200916034, 200917043–200917046, 200918022, 200918023, 200919058–200919060, 200926029, 200926031, 200926034, 200926035, 200926038,

Chapter Nine	Taxable Expenditures

200926043–200926048, 200931060, 200938031–200938033, 200939031, 200940032, 200943040, 200943041, 200944054, 200945072–200945075, 200950045, 200950046, 200950048, 200950050, 200951036, 201002045, 201002046, 201003021, 201003025, 201006033, 201009014, 201010029, 201014069–201014072, 201015034–201015036, 201016085–201016087, 201016091, 201018016–201018019, 201020023, 201020024, 201021028, 201021044, 201023066, 201024067, 201026037, 201027059, 201027060, 201028043, 201028045, 201032042, 201032043, 201045032, 201045033, 201046017, 201046018, 201047026, 201052018–201052020, 201101030, 201104047–201104050, 201106018, 201106020, 201113038, 201113039, 201114032–201114034, 201115027, 201116029, 201119037, 201120033, 201120034, 201121030, 201121031, 201122029, 201125046, 201126031–201126033, 201127012, 201128026, 201132024–201132026, 201135033, 201136028, 201138049, 201139010, 201140026, 201140027, 201143024–201143026, 201144033–201144036, 201146018, 201147036, 201147037, 201152022, 201202030–201202037, 201203026–201203029, 201204014, 201204015, 201205016–201205019, 201207010–201207012, 201208037, 201210038, 201210039, 201211027–201211029, 201214032, 201214033, 201216041–201216044, 201217023, 201217024, 201217027, 201219033, 201219034, 201220036, 201220038, 201223022, 201224038, 201224039, 201226030–201226033, 201227005, 201228038, 201232037, 201233020, 201235025, 201236031, 201239014, 201240024, 201241013, 201242013, 201245028, 201249017, 201250026, 201251020, 201251021, 201252019, 201302042, 201304009, 201304010, 201306024, 201306025, 201310042, 201310044, 201315032, 201315033, 201316022, 201316023, 201317019, 201318008, 201319032, 201319033, 201321029–201321031, 201322047, 201322048, 201324019, 201330044, 201330045, 201335021, 201335022, 201340018, 201343027, 201345035, 201348016, 201404014, 201408033, 201409011, 201410036, 201411043, 201411044, 201414030, 201415012, 201418062, 201420022, 201421025–201421027, 201422026, 201424026, 201425017, 201425018, 201426027, 201426030, 201427020–201427022, 201428010, 201430015, 201430016, 201431033, 201432023, 201432024, 201433025, 201433026, 201436052, 201436053, 201437016–201437020, 201438031, 201441022–201441027, 201442059, 201442060, 201442062, 201442063, 201444041, 201444042, 201442063, 201443022–201443028, 201446023, 201445019–201445031, 201446023, 201446027, 201447044–201447048, 201448029, 201448030, 201450024–201450027, 201450030–201450033, 201451047–201451061, 201449004, 201449005, 201449007, 201501017–201501024, 201502018, 201502019, 201504018, 201504019, 201505044, 201506012,

Chapter Nine	Taxable Expenditures

201507027–201507038, 201508012–201508020, 201509042–201509064, 201510048, 201510049, 201510052–201510054, 201510057, 201511027–201511032, 201512003, 201512005, 201514017, 201514018, 201516067, 201516068, 201516070–201516079, 201517020–201517025, 201518019, 201522008, 201522011, 201524025, 201525015–201525018, 201526017, 201527046–201527049, 201528039–201528041, 201529015, 201530023, 201533017–201533021, 201543017, 201534019, 201535020–201535024, 201536026, 201539034, 201539035, 201540018, 201541011, 201543019, 201544032, 201545032, 201548022, 201548023, 201549030, 201550045–201550048, 201606031, 201608017–201608020, 201609009, 201610022, 201612015, 201613017, 201614039, 201615020, 201617013, 201618012, 201618018, 201619011–201619014, 201620017, 201620018, 201621018, 201621019, 201622034, 201623014–201623018, 201625020, 201626026–201626028, 201627003, 201627004, 201628023, 201629010–201629012, 201630018, 201632024, 201632025, 201634027, 201634028, 201635009, 201635010, 201636047, 201636048, 201638024–201638027, 201639017, 201641028–201641030, 201642038, 201645018, 201646008, 201647011–201647013, 201648017, 201649018, 201649019, 201650021, 201651017, 201652024–201652027, 201701024, 201701025, 201701024, 201701025, 201702038, 201702045–201702047, 201703015, 201704022–201704024, 201707012, 201707013, 201708002, 201710037–201710039, 201711012, 201711013, 201711015, 201713011, 201714032–201714035, 201715005, 201716050, 201716051, 201717047, 201718041, 201718042, 201719027, 201719028, 201721023, 201726016–201726018, 201728023, 201729024, 201729026, 201731018, 201732036, 201733018, 201734011, 201736030, 201736031, 201737014, 201737015, 201742029–201742033, 201744021, 201746029, 201747010–201747012, 201748012, 201750022, 201805016, 201808021–201808023, 201809012–201809014, 201810012, 201811017, 201812018–201812021, 201814013, 201814014, 201817020, 201818019, 201818020, 201820021, 201822031, 201823007–201823009, 201824016, 201825033-201825035, 201828011, 201829024, 201830024, 201830025, 201831016, 201831017, 201833028-201833031, 201834014-201834016, 201835015, 201835016, 201836010, 201838010, 201839016, 201840009, 201840010, 201842007, 201842008, 201844014, 201846008, 201846009, 201848019-201848021, 201850022, 201850024-201850026, 201852021, 201852022, 201901008, 201902033, 201904018, 201905006, 201906015, 201906016, 201908025, 201911011-201911015, 201917009, 201919016, 201919018,

Chapter Nine	Taxable Expenditures
	201920012-201920015, 201921017, 201921018, 201923028, 201923029, 201926017–201926020, 201928017, 201928018, 201929020, 201930026, 201932018, 201933018, 201933019, 201933021, 201934009, 201935014, 201936011-201936013, 201937018-201937020, 201940012, 201941031, 201942012-201942015, 201943022-201943029, 201944013, 201945028, 201946015, 201947016-201947019, 201949020, 201950007, 201951006-201951009, 201952010, 202001026, 202002017-202002020, 202004016-202004021, 202005024, 202005026, 202006013, 202006014, 202007020, 202009029, 202009031, 202009032, 202010005, 202010006, 202010008, 202011009-202011011, 202011013, 202011014, 202014021, 202015029-202015033, 202016030, 202017029, 202017033, 202017038, 202017039, 202019030, 202019031, 202020023, 202020025, 202021021–202021023, 202023009, 202023010, 202026003, 202026004, 202032006, 202034006, 202034009, 202036006, 202037011
185	8709004, 8718004, 9151005
186	8915002, 9341030
188	8826029, 9050040, 9132047–9132049, 9148044, 9152038, 9204031, 9207041, 9230030, 9230032, 9239028, 9252027, 200026028, 200441034, 200444037–200444039, 200502045, 200509024, 200509025
197	9742036, 9802006, 9814050, 9822055, 9835047, 9848022, 199913049, 199914041, 199915060, 199916057, 199917080, 199918063, 199920042, 199923052, 199937048, 199945058, 199945059, 200030024, 200030025, 200031054, 200034035, 200038053, 200038056, 200041036, 200043048, 200127012, 200130050, 200134029, 200227039, 200230041, 200233026, 200235037, 200244022, 200250038, 200305033, 200315029, 200315033, 200341024
198	9050041
225	8542004
241	9651038
242	200517032
249	8408054, 8408062, 8714050
252	8729081, 8817005
254	9826031, 9826032
270	200010056
274	200551024
285	9818065, 199952092
294	8927030, 9013019, 9652027
335	200203069, 200551024
350	9147060, 9240001, 9336052, 39883
353	9011050
359	8646054, 8647084
362	8922068, 9019075, 9041003, 9041061, 9052025, 9052027, 199926048
366	8823088, 9051009, 9348052
370	9431054

Chapter Ten	Tax on Investment Income
39	8726004, 8802008, 9211005
83	200003055
89	8730061
93	8909066
129	9012001
162	8927030, 9203004, 9241003, 9415010, 9628029, 9651050

Chapter Eleven	Unrelated Business Activity
60	200715015
64	200637041, 201630009
65	200637041, 201630009
77	200715015
82	9853001, 199901002
118	200715015
119	200136025
186	200125096

Chapter Thirteen	Termination of Foundation Status
11	200827037–200827039
13	200219038, 200225045, 200226045, 200252092, 200324035
20	200415010
23	8812043, 9015072, 9019075, 9507040
25	8746079, 8822073, 8823050, 8836033, 9015072
27	9018032
33	8723038, 8920009, 9108037, 9108038, 9408012, 9511022, 9523007, 9823050, 200016027, 200028038, 200123069, 200123071, 200438041
43	8920009, 9008007, 9044039
44	8836033, 9008007, 9530024–9530026, 9537035–9537053, 200043053
46	9014004
51	8723038, 9823050, 199905027
56	200351031
64	200123069, 200123071, 200719012, 200719013
65	9725035, 200005037, 200009048, 200016025
67	9043028, 199933050, 200115044, 200513030, 200634038, 200635014, 200701033, 200732023

Chapter Thirteen	Termination of Foundation Status

78   200625044

149   8629062, 8629063, 8646057, 8712063, 8715049–8715050, 8722114, 8724069, 8725057, 8725093, 8728041, 8728074, 8732063, 8736034, 8736035, 8738064, 8746046, 8750078, 8752058, 8752059, 8803080, 8804011, 8813068, 8813069, 8813071, 8813073, 8817045, 8825099, 8825114, 8827029, 8827039, 8828015, 8830059, 8835019, 8841008, 8842057, 8847008, 8901038, 8901049, 8901063, 8903087, 8907053, 8917018, 8918088, 8920005, 8920006, 8920087, 8923038, 8924053, 8924088, 8924089, 8925013, 8925032, 8926068, 8931046, 8931049, 8939007, 8947059, 8948049, 8949042, 8949101, 9002066, 9002067, 9003044, 9013019, 9013075, 9019049, 9019054, 9019055, 9021059, 9022064, 9025085, 9033054, 9033055, 9038049, 9041003, 9041061, 9042024, 9042041, 9045066, 9047059, 9047067, 9051009, 9052025, 9052027, 9052030, 9103034, 9103035, 9104016, 9104028, 9104047, 9107037, 9109049, 9109050, 9109068, 9110060, 9111045, 9112027–9112029, 9114046, 9115057, 9132052, 9135051, 9138070, 9145033, 9145034, 9146036, 9147054, 9147055, 9150044, 9201030, 9304022, 9745029–9745031, 9750009–9750013, 9750015, 9750016, 9752065, 9752070, 9804061, 9805020, 9808036, 9808038, 9809061, 9813007, 9813009, 9813010, 9814046, 9814047, 9817031, 9817032, 9823042, 9826041, 9826047, 9826052, 9828034–9828037, 9830041, 9840031, 9841034, 9842063, 9846032, 9846038, 9847029, 9848031, 9850017, 9851051, 9846039, 9850017, 199905022, 199905023, 199905029, 199905030, 199906055, 199908052, 199908053, 199908055, 199908056, 199913043, 199914048, 199914049, 199918058, 199919037, 199920045, 199926049, 199929021, 199929047, 199930036, 199930050, 199932051, 199937053, 199940035, 199941052, 199943052, 199944044, 199945060, 199945061, 199950042, 200001048, 200003049, 200003056, 202017026, 200005036, 200006057, 200007034, 200007037, 200007041, 200007042, 200009049, 200009052, 200009054, 200009055, 200009060, 200009063, 200009068, 200010057, 200019043, 200020058, 200021057, 200022054, 200022055, 200022059, 200023054, 200023056, 200024053, 200027054, 200035034, 200037051, 200045036, 200045037, 200046041, 200049037, 200049038, 200050048, 200052038, 200101035, 200103076, 200103079, 200103082, 200103085, 200104032, 200104036, 200104037, 200106040, 200107037, 200107039, 200111045, 200111049, 200111050, 200115038, 200116048, 200117041, 200119056, 200119057, 200120041, 200120043, 200121080–200121082, 200124023, 200124026, 200124027, 200125092, 200125093, 200127051, 200130053, 200130054, 200133048, 200137060, 200137063, 200138029, 200148082, 200148083, 200150031, 200151052, 200151053, 200151057, 200204039, 200204042, 200204044, 200204046, 200204047, 200204053, 200205048, 200205049,

Chapter Thirteen	Termination of Foundation Status
	200206057, 200215054–200215056, 200216032, 200216033, 200220030, 200221050, 200221064, 200221065, 200221069, 200228030–200228033, 200229052, 200229053, 200233027–200233030, 200234065–200234068, 200234072, 200238048, 200238049, 200238050, 200241049, 200241056, 200242041, 200242045, 200243051, 200244024, 200244026, 200244027, 200245054, 200246035, 200247057, 200247060, 200251059, 200308049–200308052, 200333036, 200333037, 200416012, 200416013, 200433031, 200441037, 200501018, 200501019, 200524025, 200524028, 200543060, 200545048, 200545050, 200552017, 200644041, 200644050, 200708086, 200708088, 200715014, 200725043, 200736029, 200736030, 200806015, 200806016, 200808042, 200808043, 200830026, 200831034, 201007064, 201007065, 201020025, 201130006, 201132027, 201230026, 201231015, 201335019, 201345033, 201417020, 201417021, 201418060, 201427019, 201435016, 201438033, 201448026, 201513005, 201514016, 201603033, 201603034, 201606030, 201609001
160	200124024
161	200124074

Chapter Fourteen	Charitable Giving Rules
60	199925029

Chapter Fifteen	Private Foundations and Public Charities
41	8941026, 9152046, 9211002
58	8901051
74	39611
79	8944068, 9036004
85	8645075, 9019046
90	39748
92	8627054
98	8753049
108	38424
114	8822096, 8935058
116	8645075, 8647084, 8822092, 8927010, 9102034, 9102035, 9439014, 9530024–9530027, 9547013, 9551027, 9710013, 9730032

Chapter Fifteen	Private Foundations and Public Charities
121	9407005
126	8927010, 9407005
129	8910058, 9203038, 9530024–9530026, 9537035–9537053
132	8906008
137	200817040, 200818024, 200818027
146	8933050, 9022061, 9114031, 9243008
147	200508018
173	8845073
182	8645075, 8947060, 9014063, 9102034, 9192035, 9439014, 9527043, 9547013, 9551027, 9651039, 201608016, 201620016, 201621015, 201701023, 201704019, 201711014, 201729025, 201733019, 201909015, 201923027, 202023012, 202034007, 202034008
184	8807007, 8807049, 8814046, 8818041, 8822092, 8827059
188	201240036
199	39748
208	8822096
209	8817005
231	8811015, 9052055, 9212030, 9309038, 9450045, 9508031, 9510040
232	200552014
239	8627053, 8844023
244	200413015
247	8718051, 8718057
280	201124024
299	9138003
301	201131027
318	201120035
322	8601102, 8644066, 8640055, 9137043, 9411043, 199949045, 200020057
373	200752043
378	201029032
380	201019034, 201036025
388	8725056, 8747077, 8933059, 9309037, 9635030, 201424025, 39718

Chapter Sixteen	Donor-Advised Funds
31	200445024
43	200149045
47	200043053
77	200150039

Chapter Seventeen	Corporate Foundations
60	201725009

About the Author

BRUCE R. HOPKINS is the principal in the Bruce R. Hopkins Law Firm, LLC, Kansas City, Missouri. He concentrates in his practice on the representation of private foundations and other categories of tax-exempt organizations. His practice ranges over the entirety of law matters involving exempt organizations, with emphasis on the formation of nonprofit organizations, acquisition of recognition of tax-exempt status for them, the private inurement and private benefit doctrines, governance, the intermediate sanctions rules, legislative and political campaign activities issues, public charity and private foundation rules, unrelated business planning, use of exempt and for-profit subsidiaries, joint venture planning, tax shelter involvement, review of annual information returns, Internet communications developments, the law of charitable giving, and fundraising law issues.

Mr. Hopkins served as Chair of the Committee on Exempt Organizations, Tax Section, American Bar Association; Chair, Section of Taxation, National Association of College and University Attorneys; and President, Planned Giving Study Group of Greater Washington, D.C.

Mr. Hopkins is the series editor of Wiley's Nonprofit Law, Finance, and Management Series. In addition to being co-author of *The Tax Law of Private Foundations, Fifth Edition*, he is the author of *The Law of Tax-Exempt Organizations, Twelfth Edition; The Planning Guide for the Law of Tax-Exempt Organizations: Strategies and Commentaries; Bruce R. Hopkins' Nonprofit Law Library* (e-book); *Tax-Exempt Organizations and Constitutional Law: Nonprofit Law as Shaped by the U.S. Supreme Court; Bruce R. Hopkins' Nonprofit Law Dictionary; IRS Audits of Tax-Exempt Organizations: Policies, Practices, and Procedures; The Tax Law of Charitable Giving, Fifth Edition; The Tax Law of Associations; The Tax Law of Unrelated Business for Nonprofit Organizations; The Nonprofits' Guide to Internet Communications Law; The Law of Intermediate Sanctions: A Guide for Nonprofits; Starting and Managing a Nonprofit Organization: A Legal Guide, Seventh Edition; Nonprofit Law Made Easy; Charitable Giving Law Made Easy; Private Foundation Law Made Easy; 650 Essential Nonprofit Law Questions Answered; The First Legal Answer Book for Fund-Raisers; The Second Legal Answer Book for Fund-Raisers; The Legal Answer Book for Nonprofit Organizations;* and *The Second Legal Answer Book for Nonprofit Organizations.* He is the co-author, with Thomas K. Hyatt, of *The Law of Tax-Exempt Healthcare Organizations, Fourth Edition;* with Alicia M. Beck, of *The Law of Fundraising, Fifth Edition;* with David O. Middlebrook, of *Nonprofit Law for Religious Organizations: Essential Questions & Answers;* with Douglas K. Anning, Virginia C. Gross, and Thomas J. Schenkelberg, of *The New Form 990:*

Law, Policy and Preparation; also with Ms. Gross, of *Nonprofit Governance: Law, Practices & Trends*; and with Ms. Gross and Mr. Schenkelberg, of *Nonprofit Law for Colleges and Universities: Essential Questions and Answers for Officers, Directors, and Advisors*. He also writes *Bruce R. Hopkins' Nonprofit Counsel*, a monthly newsletter, published by John Wiley & Sons.

Mr. Hopkins maintains a website providing information about the law of tax-exempt organizations, at www.brucerhopkinslaw.com (click on nonprofit law center). Material posted on this site includes a current developments outline concerning this aspect of the law, discussions of his books, and various indexes that accompany his newsletter.

Mr. Hopkins received the 2007 Outstanding Nonprofit Lawyer Award (Vanguard Lifetime Achievement Award) from the American Bar Association, Section of Business Law, Committee on Nonprofit Corporations. He is listed in *The Best Lawyers in America*, Nonprofit Organizations/Charities Law 2007–2021.

Mr. Hopkins is the Professor from Practice at the University of Kansas School of Law, where he teaches courses on the law of tax-exempt organizations.

Mr. Hopkins earned his JD and LLM degrees at the George Washington University, his SJD at the University of Kansas, and his BA at the University of Michigan. He is a member of the bars of the District of Columbia and the state of Missouri.

About the Online Resources

The Tax Law of Private Foundations, Fifth Edition: 2020 Cumulative Supplement is complemented by a number of online resources.

For a list of all Wiley books by Bruce R. Hopkins, please visit www.wiley.com/go/hopkins.

Also, please visit www.wiley.com/go/privatefoundations5e2020supplement and enter the password *payout 123* to download various tables in PDF format and other documents to use alongside this fifth edition. These include the following:

- Appendix A—Sources of Law
- Appendix B—Internal Revenue Code Sections
- Table of Cases
- Table of IRS Revenue Rulings and Revenue Procedures
- Table of IRS Private Determinations Cited in Text
- Table of IRS Private Determinations Discussed in *Bruce R. Hopkins' Nonprofit Counsel*
- Table of IRS Private Letter Rulings, Technical Advice Memoranda, and General Counsel Memoranda

Cumulative Index